PERSONAL FINANCIAL FITNESS

A Practical Guide To Improve The Health of Your Wealth

Fifth Edition

Allen Klosowski, CFP

A FIFTY-MINUTE™ SERIES BOOK

CRISP PUBLICATIONS, INC.
Menlo Park, California

PERSONAL FINANCIAL FITNESS

A Practical Guide To Improve
The Health of Your Wealth

Fifth Edition

Allen Klosowski, CFP

CREDITS
Editor: **Michael G. Crisp**
Typesetting: **ExecuStaff**
Cover Design: **Fifth Street Design**
Artwork: **Ralph Mapson**

© 1989, 1993, 1997, 1999 by Crisp Publications, Inc.
Printed in the United States of America by Bawden Printing Company.

http://www.crisp-pub.com

Distribution to the U.S. Trade:

National Book Network, Inc.
4720 Boston Way
Lanham, MD 20706
1-800-462-6420

98 99 00 01   10 9 8 7 6 5 4 3 2 1

Library of Congress Catalog Card Number 98-074376
Klosowski, Allen
Personal Financial Fitness
ISBN 1-56052-552-5

This book is printed
on recyclable paper
with soy ink.

LEARNING OBJECTIVES FOR:

PERSONAL FINANCIAL FITNESS

The objectives for *Personal Financial Fitness* are listed below. They have been developed to guide you, the reader, to the core issues covered in this book.

Objectives

❑ 1) **To add to your knowledge and understanding of money management in order to invest your funds more effectively.**

❑ 2) **To help clarify long term goals and prepare for a secure retirement.**

Assessing Your Progress

In addition to the Learning Objectives, Crisp, Inc. has developed an **assessment** that covers the fundamental information presented in this book. A twenty-five item, multiple choice/true-false questionnaire allows the reader to evaluate his or her comprehension of the subject matter. An answer sheet with a chart matching the questions to the listed objectives is also available. To learn how to obtain a copy of this assessment please call: **1-800-442-7477** and ask to speak with a Customer Service Representative.

Assessments should not be used in any selection process.

ABOUT THE AUTHOR

Allen Klosowski, CFP—is a Certified Financial Planner and member of the Registry of Financial Planning Practitioners. Mr. Klosowski is a Registered Investment Advisor who has advised clients on financial matters since 1969. He regularly conducts seminars for corporations, hospital foundations, and charitable organizations.

If you wish to contact Mr. Klosowski regarding your financial situation, you may write or call:

Allen Klosowski, CFP
4400 MacArthur Boulevard
Suite 780
Newport Beach, CA 92660
(949) 752-1396
Fax: (949) 475-9430
E-mail: RoylReturn@aol.com

CONTENTS

CONTENTS (continued)

ACKNOWLEDGMENTS

I wish to thank Elwood "Chap" Chapman (the author of the national best-seller, COMFORT ZONES) for his guidance and support, which made this book possible.

A special thanks to my parents who have been a constant source of encouragement and inspiration to me.

The publisher would like to acknowledge the several individuals who reviewed various drafts of this material and thank them for their suggestions and contributions. Our special thanks to:

Charles Atwell, Kansas City, Missouri

Michael Buckhoff, Burbank, California

Robert Donaldson, Irvine, California

Michael Feder, Foster City, California

Daniel Gray, Menlo Park, California

Noel Johnson, Orlando, Florida

Maurice Kramer, Irvine, California

Edward I. McQuinston, Palo Alto, California

Gloria Mitchell, Cupertino, California

Gary Mordock, Esq., Fullerton, California

Mary Kay Voss, Bellevue, Washington

Judy Watt, Redondo Beach, California

William Wright, CFP, Irvine, California

SECTION

I

Financial Planning:
An Overview

WHAT IS PERSONAL FINANCIAL PLANNING?

Personal financial planning is nothing more than the development and implementation of a comprehensive plan to help a person achieve some specific financial goals. The idea is to focus on these goals as the starting point in a financial planning process.

In the planning process, an individual's financial affairs (i.e., investments, savings programs, insurance, retirement plans, estate plan, and so forth) should be considered as a coordinated whole, rather than on a piecemeal basis. Most financially secure people use a variety of financial instruments to achieve their goals and objectives.

Lawyers, accountants, bankers, trust officers, investment advisors, insurance agents, stock brokers, tax specialists, and financial planners can all help an individual to meet his or her specific financial objectives. In fact, most people need to deal with several professionals to receive the quality of expert advice that is needed for the most effective financial planning. This makes coordinating the advice among these experts very important.

Coordination of financial advice might be termed a "systems approach" toward meeting financial goals. Financial planning integrates the basic principles of each specialist into a cohesive approach for each individual.

Financial planning can help answer many "what ifs" in life such as:

- What if I want to purchase a more expensive home?

- What if I decide to go into business for myself?

- What if my children go to college?

- What if my spouse stops working?

- What if I decide to retire at age 55 instead of 65?

Financial planning is dynamic. The financial decisions you make will initiate various actions, each with its own consequences. These must be evaluated in an objective manner. Your personal commitment is essential. The time you invest in planning now will pay dividends later.

A GREATER NEED FOR FINANCIAL PLANNING

In today's increasingly complex world, everyone needs some financial planning. A bewildering array of investment opportunities, economic swings, and constantly changing tax laws, leads to confusion and frustration. Also, many people have some financial goals they wish to attain, but often these goals are vaguely defined.

Central to the planning process is the development of personal financial goal setting. Unfortunately, most people (even those with goals) do not follow consistent policies when making financial decisions. Instead, they react to day-to-day problems or advertising claims. Those with a financial plan are in a position to make more rational financial decisions.

Do I Need the Services of a Financial Planner?

COMPLETE THIS BRIEF SELF-ANALYSIS

	YES	NO
• Can I be objective in assessing my personal circumstances?	❏	❏
• Do I have time to keep track of my investments?	❏	❏
• Do I possess the knowledge of investments, taxation and changes in the law to make intelligent decisions?	❏	❏
• Can I avoid procrastinating when decisive action must be taken?	❏	❏

If you *cannot* answer yes to the questions listed above, you should consider the services of a financial planner. Please complete all of the exercises in this book before making a decision. More information on services offered by financial planners and whether you should use one will be provided later in this book.

THE FINANCIAL PLANNING PROCESS

Like a holistic approach to personal health, the process of providing financial fitness involves four basic steps. If you have the time, objectivity and expertise in investments, taxation, insurance, and estate planning, you can complete this four-step process on your own. However, most people find it helpful to seek the aid of various professionals to derive the most benefit from this comprehensive process.

Let's review the four-step action process:

1. **Examine:** It is important to first develop a profile of your financial health. This is accomplished by gathering and organizing your financial and personal data.

Your financial data should include a current tax return; a listing of your assets and liabilities; a breakdown of your monthly living expenses; information about your personal and company retirement plans; life, health, and casualty insurance policies you own plus any estate plan documents (wills or trusts) that you have.

Your personal data should include information on all family members; a clarification of your goals and objectives and an accurate assessment about your tolerance for risk.

2. **Diagnose:** This step should analyze the data that has been gathered to determine your strengths and weaknesses. Proven concepts and principles may then be applied to reach decisions regarding aspects of your financial situation.

For example, your cash reserves should be reviewed. Are they sufficient? Are they equal to at least three months fixed living expenses? Are you hindered by too much debt? Are your current (liquid) assets sufficient to meet all current obligations (those due within the next twelve month period)?

THE FINANCIAL PLANNING PROCESS (continued)

Also, do your investments match your stated goals and objectives? If income is your goal, would you consider a certificate of deposit or a money market account more appropriate than a portfolio of speculative stock issues?

3. **Prescribe:** This step is where specific courses of financial action are selected.

For example, if one of your objectives is to generate tax-free income, you (or your financial planner) might select an investment in a municipal bond fund. If you desired greater growth potential for a portion of your cash reserves, mutual funds or stocks might be more appropriate.

A desire to provide for your survivors in the event of your death would call for the drafting of an estate plan to meet your specific requests.

4. **Monitor:** You and/or your planner need to review your plan on a regular basis (at least annually) to make appropriate adjustments based upon changes in economic, financial and/or your personal circumstances.

This regular "follow-up" will also provide an opportunity to compare results with your goals and objectives.

Most of your time and effort will be spent in Step 1 and Step 2 of the financial planning process. Gathering personal and financial data and then evaluating your strengths, weaknesses, and needs is the foundation of solid financial planning.

S E C T I O N

II

Examine and Diagnose: Determine Your Financial Condition

EXAMINE YOUR FINANCIAL SITUATION

There are several exercises in this section designed to determine your overall financial condition. First, your financial pulse will be taken. Then, you will be asked to gather financial data regarding your income, expenditures, and your present net worth. The section will conclude with information about the types of insurance plans you have in force.

> **"YOU ARE WHAT YOU THINK."**
>
> **"THINK AND GROW RICH."**
>
> **"KNOW WHAT YOU WANT AND YOU WILL GENERALLY GET IT."**

These sayings emphasize the importance of attitude in life. Attitude is simply the way you view things—mentally and emotionally. If you are positive and progressive in your outlook, you almost certainly will get more out of life than if you are negative and defensive.

How you view financial matters generally, and money specifically, will greatly influence your financial success. To begin, take your financial pulse using the exercise on the next page. It will help inform you about your attitude and awareness of your current financial situation.

TAKING YOUR FINANCIAL PULSE

	Yes	No	I Don't Know
Do you have well-defined personal financial goals?	❑	❑	❑
Do you view your financial future with enthusiasm and confidence?	❑	❑	❑
Do you know what you are worth?	❑	❑	❑
Do you save money on a regular basis?	❑	❑	❑
Are you currently receiving any tax-free income?	❑	❑	❑
Do you have any investments that help to reduce your taxable income?	❑	❑	❑
Do you qualify for a deductible IRA contribution?	❑	❑	❑
Do you take advantage of all company sponsored savings/investment programs?	❑	❑	❑
Do you feel you have sufficient permanent life insurance coverage?	❑	❑	❑
Do you feel your estate plan (will/trust) accomplishes your family objectives?	❑	❑	❑
Does an accountant prepare your tax return?	❑	❑	❑
Do you use the services of a professional financial planner?	❑	❑	❑
Can you distinguish between spending and saving?	❑	❑	❑
Do you diversify your investments?	❑	❑	❑
Do you take full responsibility for your financial affairs?	❑	❑	❑
Do you spend less than you earn?	❑	❑	❑
Do you have a plan to retire in comfort?	❑	❑	❑
Do you avoid major credit card purchases?	❑	❑	❑
Have you planned for your children's college education?	❑	❑	❑
Are you generally satisfied with your investments?	❑	❑	❑

Total number	11–20	Weak pulse. The fitness program in this book should help.
marked No or	5–10	On the right track, but you need to improve.
I Don't Know	0–4	You are in good shape. Keep up the good work.

THINK AND GROW RICH (THE POWER OF POSITIVE THINKING)

Personal financial planning is a process designed to help you accomplish your goals. The nature of your goals and the way they are met is of critical importance in your planning process. Financial goals are never static. What may be appropriate or desirable at one point in your life may not be so a few years later. The process of financial planning is on-going. To begin, ask yourself these questions:

> 1. **Where am I now financially?**
>
> 2. **Where do I want to be in the future?**
>
> 3. **How am I going to get there?**

Keep the above three questions in mind as you begin your goal setting.

GOAL SETTING PROCESS

- Be specific— *Set target dates*
- Quantify your goals— *Use numbers*
- Visualize your goals— *Picture yourself having already attained your goal, to strengthen your resolve to succeed.*

EXAMPLE:

POOR: I want to live comfortably when I retire.

BETTER: I want to retire in 10 years (at age 62), and live in a condominium in Phoenix, Arizona with a net monthly income of $2,000.

By wording each of your goals in this manner, progress can be measured on a regular (i.e., annual) basis.

Now that you have an idea of how to properly formulate financial goals, take time to complete the exercise on the next page regarding your personal goals.

GOAL SETTING—DO IT NOW!

Goal setting is like taking a trip. To be successful, you must know where you are going before you can get there. Take a moment to list your most important financial goals:

Short term—(two years or less) (*Example:* pay off auto loan in 18 months)

- _____

- _____

Long term—(in excess of two years) (*Example:* retire in 10 years at age 55 to Florida and own a $100,000 home)

- _____

- _____

Once you have listed some key goals, next list some specific items that may help or hinder the attainment of these goals.

List three (action) items that will help you achieve the short- and long-term goals you listed on the previous page. (*Example:* start a monthly savings plan.)

- _____

- _____

- _____

List three obstacles that may impede the attainment of the short- and long-term goals you listed. (*Example:* excessive monthly credit card balances)

- _____

- _____

- _____

Goal setting is important because it makes you (and your family) examine your values and clarify them in writing; it enables you to plan ways to use available resources to reach your goals; and it puts you in charge and enables you to take control of your money and your life.

Three best selling books that deal with goal setting and the dynamics of positive daily affirmations: *Think and Grow Rich.* Napoleon Hill. *Psycho-Cybernetics.* Maxwell Maltz, M.D *The Power of Positive Thinking* Dr. Norman Vincent Peale.

THREE IMPORTANT FINANCIAL STATEMENTS

Now that your most important financial goals have been defined and you have a basic idea of what it will take to accomplish them, the following three financial exercises will help you determine your overall financial condition:

1. Completion of a **Personal Income Statement**. The income statement is simply a listing of all of your **income** and **expenses**. It enables you to see what you need to live on and how much you can allocate to savings and investments in order to accomplish your goals. Tracking your spending habits will help you formulate judgments about what is most important to you and when to shift your priorities.

2. Completion of a **Personal Balance Sheet**. This is an inventory of your financial resources. It shows what you have to work with as a starting point in the planning process.

3. Developing a **Budget**. This is a projection of **future** expenditures. It will help you control consumption (day-to-day living expenses) and teach you to save money.

Once you have completed a personal income statement, balance sheet and budget, you should review the goals you recorded on page 12 to determine if they can be accomplished with your current financial resources.

Completing these three financial exercises also has some additional benefits. The information you gather can serve as an aid in filling out credit applications, settling an estate and/or preparing your income tax return.

PERSONAL INCOME STATEMENT

The Income Statement is actually an income *and* expense statement. It summarizes where your income for a given period of time (monthly, quarterly, or annually) comes from, and how it was spent.

The Income Statement can, therefore, determine whether you are in control of your finances (showing a surplus) or if you are experiencing a cash flow crisis (showing a deficit).

On the facing page, list all of your various sources of income and expenses for a given period of time (for example, on an annual basis). For some items it will be necessary to compute an average figure based upon past records.

A completed sample Income Statement for the Charles and Barbara Thomas family can be studied on page 18. It would be a good idea to review this information before beginning work on your Income Statement.

Instructions to the Sample Income Statement

In the sample on page 18, we are using a one year period—January–December. You may use a shorter period of time, if you desire, such as a quarter of a year or a month, but an income statement for a year is a good place to start.

Have your checkbook handy. It will be of immeasurable help when you determine your expenses for a given period of time.

INCOME

Salary, wages, and bonuses—list gross amount earned.

Self-employment income—if you have your own business, list the gross income earned.

Annuities, pensions—money from company retirement plans.

Social Security—list payments for you (and your spouse, if applicable).

Alimony/Child Support—enter total amounts received.

INVESTMENT INCOME

Interest—money received from money market accounts, savings accounts, certificates of deposit, bonds, etc.

Dividends—income received from individual stocks or mutual funds.

Rental Income—the net operating profit from any income producing property you own.

Other—any miscellaneous income not covered above.

PERSONAL INCOME STATEMENT
(continued)

FIXED EXPENSES

These payments must be made with regularity and, for the most part, will not fluctuate in the amount due.

Housing—rent or home mortgage payments.

Utilities—gas, water, electric, and telephone.

Loan payment—such as for an automobile, boat, etc.

Taxes—Federal and State Income Taxes—would be listed on your company withholding statement. If self-employed, check with your accountant.

Social Security Withholding —check with your employer or accountant for the exact figures.

Property Taxes —if you own a home, check your property tax bill.

Insurance—includes premiums for all insurance in force—life, disability, medical, auto, casualty.

Other—could include financial support to parents or children.

List any other obligation(s) not enumerated above.

VARIABLE EXPENSES

Payments are, to some degree, discretionary. You may elect to reduce, increase, or eliminate them as circumstances dictate.

Food—might be a good time to examine your eating habits.

Clothing—include dry cleaning, laundry and personal effects.

Travel—includes major trips such as to Hawaii or Europe as well as weekend excursions.

Recreation—entertainment, dining out, green fees (if you play golf), etc.

Household maintenance—includes the cost of cleaning service, pool service, gardener, window washing, etc.

Transportation—all costs related to motorized vehicles—cars, motorboats, motorbikes—including gas, repairs, and license fees.

Education—cost of children's education or courses of study taken by you. Include tuition and cost of books.

Medical Expenses—all costs not covered by your medical or dental insurance policies.

Church and Charity—include cash contributions only.

Spending Money—pocket money, your weekly allowance.

Other—might also include such temporary expenses as a veterinarian's bill.

TOTAL THE FIXED AND VARIABLE EXPENSES, THEN SUBTRACT THIS TOTAL FROM YOUR TOTAL INCOME. HOPEFULLY, THERE IS A SUR-PLUS THAT CAN BE EARMARKED FOR THE ESTABLISHMENT OF A CASH RESERVE TO FUND A FUTURE PURCHASE (SUCH AS A CAR) OR INVESTMENTS.

In our sample on page 18 Charles and Barbara have a total income of $54,820. Their total (fixed and variable) expenses are $40,984. This leaves a surplus of $13,836 for the year to be invested, spent, or placed in savings.

THE INCOME STATEMENT

(SAMPLE)
INCOME (OR CASH FLOW) STATEMENT
Charles and Barbara Thomas
FOR THE PERIOD BEGINNING 1-1-XX
AND ENDING 12-31-XX

EARNED INCOME (Before Taxes)

Salary and Wages

Husband	36,000
Wife	18,000
Bonus	
Self Employment Income	
Annuities or Pensions	
Social Security Payments	
Alimony/Child Support	
• Other	

INVESTMENT INCOME

Interest	720
Dividends	100
Rental Income	
• Other	

INCOME (A) $ 54,820

FIXED EXPENSES

Housing—Rent/Mortgage	3,600
Utilities	760
Loan Payments	900
Taxes	
• Federal and State	8,713
• Social Security	3,861
• Property	650
Insurance Premiums	3,300
• Other	2,400

FIXED EXPENSES (B) $ 24,184

VARIABLE EXPENSES

Food	5,200
Clothing	3,000
Travel/Recreation	3,100
Household Maintenance	800
Transportation	1,250
Education	
Medical Expenses	250
Church and Charity	800
Spending Money	2,400
• Other	

VARIABLE EXPENSES (C) $ 16,800

TOTAL INCOME (A)	$ 54,820
LESS TOTAL EXPENSES (B + C)	$ 40,984
SURPLUS(DEFICIT)	$ 13,836

INCOME (OR CASH FLOW) STATEMENT

FOR THE PERIOD BEGINNING _____
AND ENDING _____

EARNED INCOME (Before Taxes)

Salary and Wages
   Husband   _____
   Wife   _____
Bonus   _____
Self Employment Income   _____
Annuities or Pensions   _____
Social Security Payments   _____
Alimony/Child Support   _____
• Other   _____

INVESTMENT INCOME

Interest   _____
Dividends   _____
Rental Income   _____
• Other   _____

                       INCOME (A) $ _____

FIXED EXPENSES

Housing—Rent/Mortgage   _____
Loan Payments   _____
Taxes
• Federal and State   _____
• Social Security   _____
• Property   _____
Insurance Premiums   _____
• Other   _____

              FIXED EXPENSES (B) $ _____

VARIABLE EXPENSES

Food   _____
Clothing   _____
Travel/Recreation   _____
Household Maintenance   _____
Transportation   _____
Education   _____
Medical Expenses   _____
Church and Charity   _____
Spending Money   _____
• Other   _____

          VARIABLE EXPENSES (C) $ _____

TOTAL INCOME (A) $ _____
LESS TOTAL EXPENSES (B + C) $ _____
SURPLUS(DEFICIT) $ _____

PERSONAL BALANCE SHEET

A fundamental starting point in the financial planning process is the creation of a personal **Balance Sheet**. It measures your financial condition at a given point in time. In its simplest form, a balance sheet consists of:

A. ASSETS (what you own)

B. LIABILITIES (what you owe)

C. NET WORTH (the difference between what you own and what you owe)

REMEMBER: A − B = C

Distinction Between an Income Statement and a Balance Sheet:

A Balance Sheet— Portrays your financial condition as of a given date, such as January 1, 19XX.

An Income Statement— Portrays your cash flow over a period of time. For example, from January 1, 19XX through December 21, 19XX—a one-year span.

Before completing your Balance Sheet shown on the next page, study the sample Balance Sheet drawn up for Charles and Barbara Thomas on page 24 and carefully read the Balance Sheet instructions on pages 21 to 23.

THE BALANCE SHEET

Instructions to Sample Balance Sheet

CURRENT ASSETS

Cash On Hand—include the cash in your wallet, cookie jar, and/or mattress.

Checking Account—could also be a money market account or money fund with check writing privileges. Use current balances.

Savings Account—use current balance.

Life Insurance Cash Values—to find the current guaranteed cash values of your insurance policy, turn to the table printed in the policy itself (term policies have no cash value). The figures in the table are for each $1,000 of the face amount of the policy for each year of the policy's age. You should call your insurance agent if you encounter any problems.

Stock/Bonds—check the value in a newspaper such as the Wall Street Journal. Call your broker if a stock or bond is not listed. Multiply the number of shares owned by the current price. Enter total.

Mutual Funds—follow the same procedure as for stocks and bonds. Use the net asset value (NAV) for the price per share.

U.S. Savings Bonds—use the face value of the bonds you own (assuming you will hold them until maturity).

Certificate of Deposit—list the value of the Certificate at maturity (unless you plan to withdraw the funds earlier).

REAL ESTATE/INVESTMENTS

Residence—with the aid of a realtor, obtain the sales price of comparable properties in your area. You may also arrange for a written appraisal (which will cost you money).

Use the same procedure for any other real property that you own.

For an interest in a limited partnership, use the amount of your original investment.

PERSONAL BALANCE SHEET (continued)

PERSONAL ASSETS

Automobile (or any other motorized vehicle)—obtain wholesale blue book value or compare your vehicle with others like it in the classified ads of your local newspaper.

Personal Property—includes home furnishings, clothing, etc. For such items, assume no greater value than what someone would pay you if you were to sell the items today. In the case of precious stones, silver, china or a coin collection, you may want to have such items appraised. If such items are covered under a homeowner's or renter's policy, your insurance agent may be able to help you in this regard.

RETIREMENT FUNDS

IRA—List the current value of all previous investments that you have made.

Company Salary Savings Plan (or other various retirement programs)—list the value that you are currently entitled to (your vested benefits).

Annuities—you can call your insurance agent to determine the current value or refer to the table in the policy itself.

CURRENT LIABILITIES

Unpaid Bills—list bills you know have to be paid in the next few months— an insurance premium, property tax bill, plumbing bill, department store accounts, etc.

Credit Cards—list current balance due on all charge cards.

Bank or Installment Loan—balance due within the next 12 month period. Auto loan, furniture, etc.

Residence Mortgage Loan—total of mortgage payments due within the next 12 months.

Other—might include money you owe your parents, personal friend, or business associate.

LONG TERM LIABILITIES

List the balance for all loans due in excess of 12 months. This would include the balance on various bank or installment loans as well as the balance due on your home mortgage.

NET WORTH OF CHARLES AND BARBARA THOMAS

Total Assets (A)

This is the sum total of current assets ($23,650), fixed assets—real estate/investments plus personal assets—($225,000 + $31,700 = $256,700) and retirement funds ($36,200). $23,650 + $256,700 + $36,200 = $316,550.

Total Liabilities (B)

This is the sum total of current liabilities ($6,150) and long term liabilities ($54,600). $6,150 + $54,600 = $60,750.

(A) – (B) = NET WORTH (C) OR

$316,550 – $60,750 = $255,800.

(SAMPLE)
BALANCE SHEET
(STATEMENT OF FINANCIAL CONDITION)
Charles and Barbara Thomas
CURRENT DATE March 31, 19XX

ASSETS		LIABILITIES	
CURRENT		**CURRENT LIABILITIES***	
Cash on Hand	$ 350	Unpaid Bills	550
Checking Account	1,300	Credit Cards	1,100
Savings Account	2,000	Bank or Installment Loan	900
Life Insurance Cash Values	1,500	Residence Mortgage Loan	3,600
Stocks/Bonds	2,500	• Other	
Mutual Funds	1,000	• Other	
• Other (U.S. Savings Bond)	5,000	• Other	
• Other (Cert. of Deposit)	10,000		
Total	$ 23,650	Total	$ 6,150
REAL ESTATE INVESTMENTS		**LONG TERM LIABILITIES**	
Residence	225,000	Bank or Installment Loan	5,600
Rental Income Property	—	Residence Mortgage Loan	49,000
Real Estate Limited Partnerships	—	• Other	
• Other		• Other	
• Other		• Other	
Total	$ 225,000	• Other	
		Total	$ 54,600
PERSONAL ASSETS			
Automobiles	7,500		
Furniture & Household Accessories	12,000		
Jewelry, Collections, Etc.	3,500		
• Other (Motor Home)	8,700		
• Other			
Total	$ 31,700	TOTAL LIABILITIES (B)	$ 60,750
RETIREMENT FUNDS			
IRA	7,200		
Company Salary Savings (401(k))	9,000		
Vested Pension Benefits	20,000		
Annuities	—		
• Other			
• Other			
Total	$ 36,200	NET WORTH (C)	$ 255,800
TOTAL ASSETS (A)	$ 316,550		

*PAYMENT DUE WITHIN NEXT 12 MONTH PERIOD.

BALANCE SHEET
(STATEMENT OF FINANCIAL CONDITION)

CURRENT DATE _____

ASSETS		LIABILITIES	
CURRENT		**CURRENT LIABILITIES***	
Cash on Hand	$ _____	Unpaid Bills	_____
Checking Account	_____	Credit Cards	_____
Savings Account	_____	Bank or Installment Loan	_____
Life Insurance Cash Values	_____	Residence Mortgage Loan	_____
Stocks/Bonds	_____	• Other	_____
Mutual Funds	_____	• Other	_____
• Other	_____	• Other	_____
• Other	_____		
Total	$ _____	Total	$ _____
REAL ESTATE INVESTMENTS		**LONG TERM LIABILITIES**	
Residence	_____	Bank or Installment Loan	_____
Rental Income Property	_____	Residence Mortgage Loan	_____
Real Estate Limited Partnerships	_____	• Other	_____
• Other	_____	• Other	_____
• Other	_____	• Other	_____
Total	$ _____	• Other	_____
		Total	$ _____
PERSONAL ASSETS			
Automobiles	_____		
Furniture & Household Accessories	_____		
Jewelry, Collections, Etc.	_____		
• Other (Motor Home)	_____		
• Other	_____		
Total	$ _____	TOTAL LIABILITIES (B)	$ _____
RETIREMENT FUNDS			
IRA	_____		
Company Salary Savings (401(k)	_____		
Vested Pension Benefits	_____		
Annuities	_____		
• Other	_____		
• Other	_____		
Total	$ _____		
TOTAL ASSETS (A)	$ _____	NET WORTH (C)	$ _____

_____

*PAYMENT DUE WITHIN NEXT 12 MONTH PERIOD.

BUDGETING

A **budget** is a worksheet that describes your lifestyle (or standard of living).

Your budget is to your financial fitness program what your diet is to your physical fitness program. The primary objective of a budget is to improve your situation in the future with a system of **disciplined** spending.

To understand where you now are financially, where you are going and how you are going to get there, complete the income and expense worksheet on page 29 after reviewing the sample budget on page 28.

REMEMBER

INCOME STATEMENT—A REPORT ON YOUR PAST

BALANCE SHEET   **—A PICTURE OF THE PRESENT**

BUDGET   **—A PLAN FOR YOUR FUTURE**

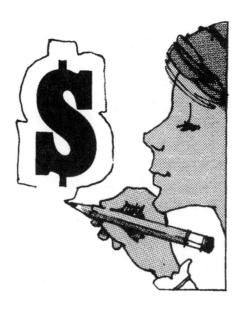

BUDGET: PART I
INCOME FORECASTING

For purposes of forecasting, figure all sources of your income on a monthly basis. Then, forecast your average monthly income over the next year by completing the worksheets shown on the next two pages.

Use the following guidelines in the completion of this income forecast:

1. Enter the monthly income for each of the various categories listed.

2. Enter the total for each month at the bottom of the page.

3. Enter the total in each income category for the year in Column "A."

4. Divide Column "A" by 12 and enter the average for each month in Column "B."

Instructions for Income Forecasting Sheet

Income forecasting is the first step in the budgeting process. On this sheet, you are to list all sources of income and when you anticipate receiving such income.

Wages or Salary—If paid monthly, list the gross amount of income.

Bonuses or Commissions—If you know you will receive a bonus a certain time of the year, list the anticipated amount in the appropriate monthly column.

Interest and Dividends—Record the amounts and months when such income is anticipated.

Rental Income—May vary from month to month.

Annuities, pensions, social security—are usually paid monthly.

Other—List any other income not previously mentioned.

Before entering your figures for the Budget Worksheets Part I found on page 29, review carefully the completed forms for Charles and Barbara Thomas on page 28.

(SAMPLE)
BUDGET: PART I
Charles and Barbara Thomas

INCOME FORECASTING
DATE March 31, (year)

Source	Jan.	Feb.	Mar.	Apr.	May	June	July	Aug.	Sept.	Oct.	Nov.	Dec.	Estimated 12-Month Total "A"	Monthly Average "B"
Husband's wages or salary	3,000	3,000	3,000	3,000	3,000	3,000	3,000	3,000	3,000	3,000	3,000	3,000	36,000	3,000
Wife's wages or salary	1,500	1,500	1,500	1,500	1,500	1,500	1,500	1,500	1,500	1,500	1,500	1,500	18,000	1,500
Bonuses or commissions														
Interest Income	60	60	60	60	60	60	60	60	60	60	60	60	720	60
Dividends			50						50				100	8
Rental Income														
Annuities, pensions, Social Security														
Other														
TOTAL BY MONTH	4,560	4,560	4,560	4,610	4,560	4,560	4,560	4,560	4,610	4,560	4,560	4,560	54,820	4,568

BUDGET: PART I

INCOME FORECASTING

DATE _____

Source	Jan.	Feb.	Mar.	Apr.	May	June	July	Aug.	Sept.	Oct.	Nov.	Dec.	Estimated 12-Month Total "A"	Monthly Average "B"
Husband's wages or salary														
Wife's wages or salary														
Bonuses or commissions														
Interest Income														
Dividends														
Rental Income														
Annuities, pensions, Social Security														
Other														
TOTAL BY MONTH														

This form may be photocopied for personal use.

BUDGET: PART II
EXPENSE FORECASTING

If you wish to keep the same lifestyle as in previous months—at least in some categories—review your past expenditures (see your completed Income or Cash Flow Statement). You can then better estimate what amounts to enter in your Budget: Part II.

Use the following guidelines in the completion of this expense forecast:

1. For categories such as medical insurance premiums, write in the amount if you pay it, or write "paid by employer," if that is applicable. Similarly, for taxes, you may write "withheld by employer."

2. Enter monthly expenses for each of the categories listed.

3. Enter a total for each month at the bottom of the page.

4. Enter the total in each expense category for the year in Column A.

5. Divide Column A by 12 and enter the average for each month in Column B.

As earlier, it would be helpful to look at the completed worksheets for Charles and Barbara Thomas (page 33) before beginning work on yours.

POINTS TO PONDER

Can the total monthly spending be accommodated by your average monthly income? If not, start making some priority decisions. Where can you make adjustments? What (variable) expenditures can be postponed or reduced? Remember, the budgeting process will require sacrifice and compromises. It is best to resolve any potential deficits before the money is actually spent.

Instructions to Sample Expense Forecasting

► **Housing—Rent/Mortgage Payments**

Reflect any future increase or decrease due to a move, refinancing, etc.

► **Housing—Repairs/Improvements**

You may wish to include a figure in Column A which will serve as a contingency fund or reserve.

► **Utilities**

Includes gas, electric, water, and telephone. Make seasonal adjustments for increased air conditioning or heating needs.

► **Food**

Also include household items such as paper towels, soap, pet food, etc.

► **Medical**

Premiums. If coverage is provided by your employer, write "Covered by Employer."

► **Medical—Doctor, Dentist, Drugs and Hospital**

You may wish to put a total in Column A serving as a contingency or reserve fund. This would cover the deductible and co-insurance factor contained in your medical policy.

► **Clothing**

If you are fairly consistent in the amount that you spend, fill in an average monthly figure. Otherwise, establish a reserve fund in Column A.

► **Transportation**

You may wish to average the costs on a monthly basis. In the example on page 33, we are showing quarterly insurance premium payments. Include monthly charges for gas, oil, and repairs. A review of previous records should give you a fairly accurate monthly figure.

BUDGET: PART II EXPENSE FORECASTING (continued)

► **Recreation/Entertainment**

You will note the June figure (page 33) is substantially higher than the other months. This is in anticipation of a vacation in June.

► **Personal Improvement**

List all magazine subscriptions, health club dues, tuition, etc.

► **Short Term Funding**

If you are currently paying for major household items such as a refrigerator, list the monthly payments you are making.

► **Savings and Investment**

In our example on page 33, the Thomases are making an IRA contribution in April, and plan to invest $8,654 in the month of December. If you are on a systematic investment program, put in your monthly figure.

► **Spending Money**

Record the amount of cash you carry and spend monthly.

► **Gifts**

If a family wedding is anticipated or a special birthday celebration, estimate the costs of that specific occasion. Otherwise, a monthly average figure should be used.

► **Church and Charity**

Indicate the frequency of contributions that are made. In the sample, the Thomases elect to make cash contributions twice a year, once in June and once in December.

► **Life Insurance**

List all premium payments (monthly, quarterly, etc.).

► **Taxes**

If Federal and State Income Taxes are withheld by your employer, write "Withheld by Employer" and record the total.

► **Miscellaneous**

List any other anticipated expense not enumerated above.

(SAMPLE)
BUDGET: PART II
Charles and Barbara Thomas

EXPENSE FORECASTING
DATE March 31, (year)

Expense Category	Explanation of Categories	Jan.	Feb.	Mar.	Apr.	May	June	July	Aug.	Sept.	Oct.	Nov.	Dec.	Estimated 12 Month Total "A"	Monthly Average "B"
Housing	Rent, mortgage payments, insurance and taxes	579	579	579	579	579	579	579	579	579	579	579	579	6,948	579
	Repairs and improvements														
Utilities	Gas, electric, water, telephone	63	63	63	63	63	63	63	63	63	63	63	63	756	63
Food		433	433	433	433	433	433	433	433	433	433	433	433	5196	433
Medical	Premiums	COVERED BY EMPLOYER													
	Doctor, dentist, drugs and hospital													600*	50
Clothing														3,000*	250
Transportation (all motorized vehicles)	Purchase payments, insurance and license fees			250			250			250			250	1,000	83
	Gas, oil, repairs, parking, tolls and so on	104	104	104	104	104	104	104	104	104	104	104	104	1,248	104
Recreation and entertainment	Dining out, movies, vacations, etc.	92	92	92	92	92	2,092	92	92	92	92	92	92	3,104	259
Personal improvement	Magazines and newspapers														
	Books and tuition														
Short-term funding	Purchase of a major appliance														
Savings and investment	For long-term goals: IRAs, Annuities, Stocks, Bonds, Mutual Funds				2,000								8,654	10,654	888
Spending money	Cash carried in wallet	200	200	200	200	200	200	200	200	200	200	200	200	2,400	200
Gifts	Weddings, birthdays, etc.						400						400	800	67
Church and charity															
Life insurance		45	45	45	45	45	45	45	45	45	45	45	45	540	45
Taxes		WITHHELD BY EMPLOYER												12,574	1,048
Miscellaneous	Legal services, debt repayments, union dues, etc.	500	500	500	500	500	500	500	500	500	500	500	500	6,000	500
TOTAL		2,016	2,016	2,266	4,016	2,016	4,666	2,016	2,016	2,266	2,016	2,016	11,320	54,820*	4,568

* A contingency fund for the year.

** Total By Month—January–December = $51,220

+Contingency funds (medical/clothing) + 3,600

Estimated 12 Month Total "A" $54,820

BUDGET: PART II

EXPENSE FORECASTING

DATE _____

Expense Category	Explanation of Categories													Estimated 12 Month Total "A"	Monthly Average "B"
Housing	Rent, mortgage payments, insurance and taxes														
	Repairs and improvements														
Utilities	Gas, electric, water, telephone														
Food															
Medical	Premiums														
	Doctor, dentist, drugs and hospital														
Clothing															
Transportation (all motorized vehicles)	Purchase payments, insurance and license fees														
	Gas, oil, repairs, parking, tolls and so on														
Recreation and entertainment	Dining out, movies, vacations, etc.														
Personal improvement	Magazines and newspapers														
	Books and tuition														
Short-term funding	Purchase of a major appliance														
Savings and investment	For long-term goals: IRAs, Annuities, Stocks, Bonds, Mutual Funds														
Spending money	Cash carried in wallet														
Gifts	Weddings, birthdays, etc.														
Church and charity															
Life insurance															
Taxes															
Miscellaneous	Legal services, debt repayments, union dues, etc.														
TOTAL															

This form may be photocopied for personal use.

THE ROLE OF INSURANCE IN FINANCIAL PLANNING

The fundamental objective of insurance is to provide a means to offset the burden of financial loss. Think of insurance as an alternative method of dealing with risk. You are paying an insurance premium (small cost) to avoid paying the total cost for a catastrophic loss (such as your house burning down).

A sound insurance program should answer the "what ifs" in your life. For example:

What if you were faced with a major medical expense or nursing home confinement? (health and long-term care insurance)

What if you were unable to work for a long period of time due to a severe illness or accident? (disability insurance)

What if someone injured themselves on your property? (homeowner's insurance)

What if a fire destroyed many of your personal possessions? (homeowner's insurance)

What if you were involved in a severe automobile accident? (auto insurance)

What if you were to die tomorrow? (life insurance)

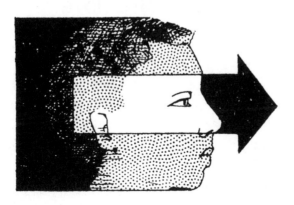

THE ROLE OF INSURANCE IN FINANCIAL PLANNING (continued)

Insurance affects everyone. Few people could own their own home, drive a car, attain adequate medical attention or provide financial security for their family without it. By providing the means to help people accomplish their goals without fear of catastrophic loss, insurance can improve the quality of life. It is, therefore, important to be aware of the major types of insurance coverage.

Life Insurance—provides a lump sum payment (or sometimes a series of payments) in the event of the death of the family breadwinner.

Disability Insurance—provides a monthly income benefit in the event the family breadwinner is disabled (unable to work) because of an accident or long term illness.

Medical (health) Insurance—provides for coverage in the event of hospitalization and medical expenses arising from injury or sickness.

Property, Casualty, and Liability Insurance—provides protection from the claims of others as well as the loss of personal property. Most typical policies are automobile and homeowners/renters. Each provides a variety of coverages.

Long-Term Care (LTC) Insurance—Skilled, intermediate or custodial care in a nursing home facility or home confinement. (For those 50 to 80 years old)

Please take the time to complete the insurance checklist on page 37 and then review all of your various insurance policies (both personal and group—those provided by your employer). Then complete the worksheet on page 45. The intent is to make you aware of the types of insurance coverage you have in force. Don't spend time analyzing each policy, but do record the basic information on each.

AUTHOR'S NOTE

When you meet with an insurance agent to review your insurance program, you should:

- ask about an umbrella policy—one which offers coverage after the limits of your automobile and/or homeowner's/renter's policies have been exhausted.

- discuss premium savings that would occur if you increased your deductibles.

- ask how to protect yourself from uninsured or underinsured motorists.

INSURANCE CHECKLIST

To help you focus on your insurance needs, complete the following checklist.

Yes   No

❑   ❑   I am aware of and have considered the four basic forms of insurance protection:

- Life — Protection against financial disruption in the event of my death, or that of my spouse.

- Disability — Protection against the loss of my ability to produce income (economic death).

- Medical and long term care (health) — Protection against prolonged illness or severe injury.

- Property, Casualty & Liability — Protection against personal losses, lawsuits, & liability— property damage, and automobile accidents.

❑   ❑   I have given some thought to the four basic methods of managing risk.

- Avoidance of risk — If I don't drive a car, I can't be the driver involved in a traffic accident.

- Reduction or prevention of risk — If I remove combustible materials from my garage, I minimize the risk of fire.

- Assumption or retention of risk — I assume greater risk by choosing a larger deductible for my insurance policy. (The trade off is a lower premium rate.)

- Transfer of risk — If I buy insurance, the insurance company would incur all losses once the deductible has been satisfied.

❑   ❑   I plan to evaluate annually:

- All of my insurance coverage to prevent gaps or duplication.

- To replace or update policies on the basis of cost and coverage.

LIFE INSURANCE: A FLEXIBLE MONEY INSTRUMENT

What Life Insurance Provides

Life insurance is the only instrument that can provide living benefits or become self-completing upon death. Life insurance is an important part of your total financial picture.

Life insurance provides a source of instant and tax-free liquidity (income). Such liquidity is very important in the early stages of family and economic development and can also help protect accumulated wealth in later years by providing an instant source of (tax-free) cash.

Two Basic Kinds of Life Insurance

▶ **TERM**—Provides protection only for a specified term or period of time. The policy pays off only in the event you die. It is the cheapest form of insurance protection in terms of initial premium payments, but not necessarily the most cost effective form of insurance in the long run.

▶ **PERMANENT**—Protection is provided for the lifetime of the insured. Other names for permanent insurance include: whole life, interest sensitive, or universal life insurance. Such policies have a cash value (savings) feature. The cash values accumulate on a tax deferred basis at a very competitive rate—currently 8–10%. The present-day policies are structured to allow the premiums to "vanish" in a relatively short period of time—approximately 10 years.

BENEFITS OF CASH VALUE-ORIENTED LIFE INSURANCE

- Cash values accumulate tax free—usually at a very competitive interest rate.

- The owner may borrow funds from the policy on a tax-free basis (given certain circumstances under current legislation).

- The death benefit is paid to the beneficiary free of income taxes.

- The death benefit avoids probate.

- Limited number of premium payments based upon age and the amount of insurance applied for.

LIFE AND DEATH BENEFITS OF CASH VALUE INSURANCE

To demonstrate both the life and death benefits of the present-day insurance policies, consider the case of Jason White who is 45 years old. He has a wife and three young children.

Jason wants an insurance plan that will provide ample protection for his family and the opportunity for supplemental income beginning at age 65.

His cash flow will allow him to spend approximately $200 a month for premiums, which will provide the following policy:

SUMMARY OF BENEFITS:

- The initial amount of insurance purchased is $200,000.00

- Jason will pay a total premium over a 20-year period of $48,000.00

- Beginning at age 65 and for each of the next 20 years, he can withdraw $2,000 income *tax free* for a total of $40,000.00

- At age 85, the net death benefits would be $160,000.00

- The net amount of cash remaining in the policy at age 85 would be $52,000.00

AUTHOR'S NOTE

To obtain a detailed insurance illustration, you should contact your insurance agent or financial advisor.

Tax Fact

As a result of the Technical and Miscellaneous Revenue Act of 1988 (TMRA 88), all Single Premium Whole Life policies issued after June 20, 1988, will continue to receive tax deferred accumulations, a tax free death benefit, but not tax free policy loans. Any withdrawals will be treated as ordinary income. Furthermore, these distributions will be subject to a 10% penalty if taken prior to age 59 ½.

LIFE INSURANCE—BUSINESS PLANNING APPLICATIONS

Pension and Profit Sharing Plans—Qualified Retirement Plans—are burdened with a crushing load of rules and regulations. The strict compliance rules and administrative costs associated with such plans can be avoided through the use of a Whole Life or Universal Life Insurance Policy.

Advantages of using life insurance:

- Like funds in a retirement plan, the premiums paid to the insurance company build up tax free.

- If an employee dies prior to retirement, the policy pays off as a non-taxable death benefit.

- Payments to a retired employee by a qualified retirement plan are fully taxable, but withdrawals from a life insurance policy can be tax free by borrowing the accumulated cash values.

Application #1: Traditional Split Dollar Insurance

SITUATION: Alex is a Vice President for Vortex, a small paper company. He has expressed a desire to have more life insurance protection for his family.

SOLUTION: Vortex can purchase a life insurance contract (with a vanishing premium) on Alex's life. Vortex pays the bulk of the premium (equal to the annual cash value build-up). Alex is the owner of the policy. Alex's beneficiaries would receive the policy's proceeds (less all premiums paid by the company) in the event of his death while still employed. Alex would pay a small cost for the insurance based upon either IRS set rates or the insurance company's standard term insurance rate.

Application #2: Reverse Split Dollar Situation

SITUATION: John works for a small manufacturing company that has a modest pension plan. The company would like to increase John's retirement benefits, but because of anti-discrimination laws, can't increase his benefits without raising the benefits of everyone on the payroll.

SOLUTION: The company agrees to pay the premiums for an insurance contract with John as the insured and owner of the policy (including all of the accumulated cash values).

The company will be the beneficiary during John's working years. The policy can be structured so that by the time John retires, the premiums will have vanished. The beneficiary is then changed to John's designee. John would thus have accumulated cash values to supplement his retirement income.

Application #3: Deferred Compensation Situation

SITUATION: Mark is a highly salaried Executive Vice President for a large publicly traded corporation. He does not need all of his annual income and would like to reduce his current income tax liability.

The company would like to reward Mark for his contributions to the company as a key employee. A supplemental executive retirement plan has been considered.

SOLUTION: The company enters into a formal agreement with Mark to defer a portion of his annual income (say, $10,000). In conjunction with this agreement, a life insurance contract is purchased on the life of Mark by the company. If Mark dies while employed, his beneficiaries receive the death benefit, tax free. When Mark retires, he receives the cash values from the insurance contract to supplement other retirement income. In effect, the amount of retirement income paid out is equal to the amount of money deferred.

HOW TO CALCULATE YOUR LIFE INSURANCE NEEDS

1. **Annual Living Expenses** of
   Survivors (spouse, children, etc.) $_____
   (Consider using 70% of current family living expenses)

2. **Less Expected Annual Benefits**
   A. Social Security Benefits $_____
   B. Pension Survivor Benefits $_____
   C. Annuities $_____
   Total Expected Annual Benefits $_____

3. **Net Living Expense Shortage** $_____
   (Line 1 minus Line 2)

4. **Amount of Capital Required** to
   Produce Living Expense Shortage $_____
   (Line 3 divided by projected rate of return on invested
   capital. Consider using a conservative return rate to
   adjust for inflation.   _____

   Inflation-adjusted Rate of Return   _____%

5. **PLUS Other Lump Sum Expenses**
   A. Death Transfer Costs $_____
   B. Mortgage Cancellation $_____
   C. Education Fund or Other $_____
   D. Emergency Fund $_____
   Total Lump Sum Expenses $_____

6. **Total Capital Required** $_____

7. **LESS Present Capital**
   A. Income Producing Assets $_____
   B. Present Life Insurance $_____
   Total Present Capital $_____

8. **Amount of Capital to be Added (Insurance)**, if any
   (Difference between Lines 6 and 7) $_____

LONG-TERM CARE (LTC)

What Is Long-Term Care?

Long-Term care is the service and support required for day-to-day living when an accident, a prolonged illness, or even frailty prevents you from caring for yourself. Such care can range from professional care in a nursing home to help with day-to-day living activities in your own home.

Who Pays for Long-Term Care?

A 1992 study sponsored by the Health Care Financing Administration, the government agency that administers Medicare, concluded that Medicare paid for only 10% of all Long-Term Care costs.

Only when an individual becomes financially indigent, will a state government provide the day-to-day care that is needed.

Why You Should Consider Long-Term Care Protection

A study reported by the New England Journal of Medicine in 1992 anticipates that 43% of people over the age of 65 will enter a nursing facility during their lifetime. The average cost of a one-year stay in such a facility is estimated to be over $30,000 annually.

Long-Term Care Insurance is the most efficient means of protecting your assets and income from this threat. If you purchase such an insurance policy, you not only protect assets and income, but provide peace of mind for yourself and other family members. Such protection will also increase your independence and control over future care needs.

LONG-TERM CARE (LTC) (continued)

Benefits Provided by Individual Long-Term Care Policy:

- Home Health Services
- Professional Care Services
- Homemaker Services
- Adult Day Care Services
- Hospice Care Services

- Convalescent Home Care
- Home Modification
- Medical Alert System
- Caregiver Training
- Therapeutic Devices

Cost of Long-Term Care Insurance

A policy can be structured to provide waiver of premium, a spousal discount, a paid-up policy for the surviving spouse, and a return of premium rider upon death of one of the spouses.

Benefits can be altered to meet your cash flow requirements.

You should contact a Certified Financial Planner or Insurance Agent for an illustration setting forth the benefits and costs.

INSURANCE COVERAGE SUMMARY

List the amount of insurance protection provided by each policy.

LIFE INSURANCE COVERAGE	(Self)	(Spouse)	Annual Cost
Company Group Life Insurance	$_____	$_____	$_____
Travel Accident Insurance	_____	_____	_____
Accidental Death & Dismemberment Insurance (AD&D)	_____	_____	_____
Personal Life Insurance	_____	_____	_____
Policy #_____	_____	_____	_____
Policy #_____	_____	_____	_____
Policy #_____	_____	_____	_____
TOTAL	_____	_____	_____

DISABILITY COVERAGE

Group Long Term Disability

Individual Disability Programs			
Policy #_____	_____	_____	_____
Policy #_____	_____	_____	_____

MEDICAL (OR LTC) COVERAGE			
Company Medical Plan—Self	_____	_____	_____
Company Medical Plan—Spouse	_____	_____	_____
Individual Medical or LTC Coverage	_____	_____	_____
Policy #_____	_____	_____	_____
Policy #_____	_____	_____	_____

HOMEOWNERS/RENTERS COVERAGE			
Personal Property	_____	_____	_____
Fire	_____	_____	_____
Liability	_____	_____	_____
Policy #_____	_____	_____	_____

AUTO COVERAGE			
Liability	_____	_____	_____
Collision	_____	_____	_____
Comprehensive	_____	_____	_____
Other	_____	_____	_____
Policy #_____	_____	_____	_____

S E C T I O N

III

An R$_X$ for Investment and Tax Planning

MAKING YOUR MONEY WORK FOR YOU

You have just completed Step 1 (Examine) and Step 2 (Diagnose) in the financial planning process. You are now ready for Step 3 (Prescribe). The concepts and principles of investing discussed in this section may be considered a prescription to aid in the improvement of your financial health.

No one financial prescription is right for everyone, just as no single medical prescription can be applied with equal results. Once a recommended action is taken, it is important to monitor the results (Step 4) and make any adjustments that may be necessary on a regular basis.

> An I.D.E.A.L. investment portfolio would contain the following prescribed ingredients:
>
> - Income (bank account interest; stock dividends; municipal bond interest)
>
> - Deductions (an IRA; your home mortgage interest payment)
>
> - Equity buildup (mortgage reduction on your home or income producing property)
>
> - Appreciation (increase in stock or mutual fund prices)
>
> - Liquidity (easily convertible to cash in an emergency—money market funds, savings accounts, stocks)

MAKING YOUR MONEY WORK FOR YOU (continued)

Everyone would like a good return on his or her investments. What constitutes a good return depends on several things: your personal circumstances, your tolerance for risk, and the characteristics of a given investment (such as liquidity, capital appreciation or tax deferral).

There is no single best or perfect investment. Each has strengths and weaknesses that must be considered in light of your particular needs. For example, you must consider whether you are willing to risk a loss of principal for the possibility of a higher gain.

The two basic categories of investments are growth and income. Generally there is more risk associated with growth-oriented investments (i.e., a share of stock) than with income-oriented investments (i.e., savings account).

Income-oriented prescriptions (i.e., R_χs) would include: U.S. government securities, corporate and municipal bonds, single-premium deferred annuities, savings accounts, income mutual funds, money market funds, and certificates of deposit.

Growth-oriented R_χs would include: stocks, variable annuities, growth mutual funds, and real estate.

Speculative investments (which offer growth opportunities but also substantial risk) include: commodity trading (precious metals, pork bellies, etc.), equipment leasing, research & development programs, raw land, oil and gas exploration and some types of limited partnerships.

REMEMBER: Normally the greater the potential reward (gain), the greater the risk.

CAVEAT: Always obtain and read the prospectus (disclosure of investment information) before making your final decision on any investment.

The basic objective of investing is to earn the maximum possible rate of return on the funds you have to invest, that is consistent with your goals, objectives, and tolerance for risk. The following pages contain information about factors that will influence your investment decisions.

SEVEN FACTORS INFLUENCING YOUR INVESTMENT DECISIONS

A doctor, when diagnosing an ailment, must look at all the symptoms before prescribing the right medication. Conversely, before a specific investment can be selected (prescribed), you must consider its primary objective—income or growth—in light of your specific goals and your tolerance for risk.

Listed below are seven factors to consider before making an investment decision. After you have finished reading them, rate the factors in order of their importance to you with 1 being "Most Important" and 7 being "Least Important." Place a number in the box provided.

1. *Safety of Principal (Original Investment Capital) and Income*

To determine the relative safety of any investment, you must first analyze four types of risk:

Financial Risk—Unfavorable business conditions may reduce or eliminate an expected return (i.e., a company in which you owned a number of shares goes bankrupt).

Market Risk—Price fluctuations due to changes in investor attitudes (i.e., your utility stock goes down because of the Three Mile Island scare).

Interest Rate Risk—Market prices for your bonds (fixed income securities) tend to move inversely with changes in the general level of interest rates—as interest rates rise, bond prices fall.

Purchase Power Risk—The negative effect of inflation on the future purchasing power of your investments (i.e., the earnings of your savings account are not an adequate hedge against inflation).

Are you willing to take greater risks for the possibility of a greater reward? It's important to understand (when making investment decisions) your tolerance for risk taking. How much investment risk are you willing to take?

Low _____ Moderate _____ High _____

Is the risk you are willing to take in keeping with your objectives?

SEVEN FACTORS INFLUENCING YOUR INVESTMENT DECISIONS (continued)

☐ **2.** *Rate of Return—The Yield or Amount You Earn on Your Investment*

- Your yield can come from a variety of investment returns, such as interest, dividends, rental income, or capital appreciation.

- Normally, the greater your yield, the greater your risk.

☐ **3.** *Taxation of Income—Your Yield after Taxes*

Taxes and investments are interrelated. Just as you control your weight to maintain good health, you can control to a large degree the amount of taxes that you pay with your investment strategies. Your investment choices will ultimately determine the taxes you pay or don't pay. It is the marginal tax rate (i.e., an individual's tax bracket) that often influences an investment decision.

For example, current yield (8%) multiplied by 100% minus your highest income tax bracket (30%) equals after-tax yield.

> **OR:**
>
> $0.08 \times (1.00 - .30)$
>
> $= 0.08 \times (.70)$
>
> $= .056$ or 5.6% return on your 8% current yield
>
> *IT'S WHAT YOU GET TO KEEP THAT COUNTS.*

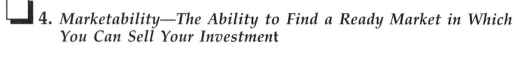

4. *Marketability—The Ability to Find a Ready Market in Which You Can Sell Your Investment*

For example, common stocks are easily sold; selling real estate is often slower and more difficult, as is the sale of a business.

5. *Liquidity—The Ability to Find a Ready Market for Your Investment and Stability of the Price You Will Receive*

The key is to get your money back, quickly and easily, without incurring a loss. You would expect to receive all of your original investment from a savings account, but probably less if you sold a volatile stock in a declining market.

6. *Diversification—A Defensive or Conservative Investment Policy Designed to Reduce Your Risk of Loss*

For example, you can:

—Diversify among several types of investments—real estate, common stocks and certificates of deposit.

—Diversify within a particular type of investment—buy several different common stock issues.

—Diversify according to maturity—buy bonds and certificates of deposit that have different maturity dates.

—Diversify the timing of investments—rather than investing a lump sum, invest a small amount every month (systematic investing).

SEVEN FACTORS INFLUENCING YOUR INVESTMENT DECISIONS (continued)

7. *Ease of Management—The Avoidance of Worry over Fluctuations in Your Investment Results*

You may want to eliminate time and work involved in managing your investment. For example, a mutual fund offers professional management and diversification. This is not true if you own your own apartment complex that you personally manage.

WHAT IS YOUR INVESTMENT RISK TOLERANCE?

QUALIFIED RETIREMENT PLANS

One of the principal sources of retirement income, aside from social security, is from the retirement plans adopted by either a large corporation or small business owner.

Qualified plans by definition offer the following advantages:

- Plan deposits (contributions) are deductible as a business expense. This is a strong motivation to establish a retirement plan.

- Plan contributions are not currently taxable to employees, including owners/employers.

- All funds, both contributions and earnings, accumulate tax free.

- The income is taxed only as it is received (hopefully, when the employee is in a lower tax bracket).

If you are an employee of a corporation:

	YES	NO
1. Does your company offer any of the qualified plans listed on pages 56–57?	❏	❏
2. If so, are you an active participant (either making voluntary contributions or having them made for you by the company) of the plan?	❏	❏
3. Do you receive an annual valuation of your account balance in writing?	❏	❏
4. Do you know the projected value (in monthly income) at the time of your retirement?	❏	❏
5. If you are near retirement, do you understand the alternative ways of receiving your funds and the resultant tax consequences?	❏	❏

AUTHOR'S NOTE

Consult your employer regarding specific plan information. Most large corporations have an Employee Benefits section which handles the administration of all company retirement plans.

You may wish to consult your tax advisor or financial planner to determine the tax consequences of the various options available to you.

QUALIFIED PLANS

Plan	Description	Maximum Annual Contributions
IRA	Individual Retirement Account*	$2,000 or 100% of compensation, whichever is less ($2,000 for a non-working spousal IRA)
SEP	Simplified Employee Pension Consists of IRA's established by the employer for the employees Employer contributions are discretionary; same percentages must be allocated to each participant	15% of compensation or $24,000, whichever is less
TSA	Tax Shelter Annuity A retirement plan for employees of public school systems or nonprofit organizations Funds are invested in life company annuity contracts	$10,000 or 25% of compensation, whichever is less (Amount increases annually) Additional contributions allowable based upon length of employment and special catch-up provisions
401(k)	Employee sponsored savings plan Both employer and employee contributions are allowable Employer may match a certain portion of employee contributions. Percentage must be the same for all participants	Employee contribution is lesser of 25% of compensation or $10,000 (Amount increases annually) Maximum allocation (which includes any employer contributions) to any participant is the less of $30,000 or 25% of the participant's compensation
Defined Contribution	A profit-sharing plan Annual employer contributions can vary—0 to 15% Percentage contributed by the employer must be the same for each employee	15% of compensation or $24,000, whichever is less

Defined Benefit	A pension plan	100% of compensation or $160,000, whichever is less
	The amount of income received at retirement is guaranteed by the plan	
	An actuary is required to determine the actual contribution needed each year	
Money Purchase Pension Plan	Allows for a higher percentage of contribution than the profit-sharing plan	25% of compensation or $30,000, whichever is less
	Once the contribution percent is selected, the employer must contribute the same percentage each year, regardless of company profits	
Combined Profit Sharing and Money Purchase Plan	The employer can either contribute the full combined percentage of 25% or opt only for the required 10% of the Money Purchase Plan	25% of compensation or $30,000, whichever is less
	The profit-sharing contribution remains discretionary each year with a maximum of 15% of compensation	

The Tax Relief Act of 1997 created 3 additional IRAs—Non-Deductible, Roth, and Educational. Ask your Financial Advisor for specifics relating to each newly created account.

QUALIFIED PLANS (continued)

IRA Rollover: A Flexible Retirement Planning Tool

What Is It?

A rollover is simply a transfer of money from one place to another. The IRA rollover account is also known as a Self-Directed Trust. Such an account or trust is established by you in your name. You may place into this account prior IRA contributions and your vested company retirement funds from such programs as the 401(k), ESOP, PAYSOP, profit-sharing plan and pension plan.

As long as you rollover your funds into the Self-Directed Trust within sixty (60) days of the date of distribution from the previous plan(s), you avoid paying taxes on the funds. All earnings on the funds in the Self-Directed Trust accumulate and compound tax free. No taxes are paid until money is withdrawn from the account. Withdrawals are subject to ordinary income taxation.

You control the account. You make all investment and withdrawal decisions. Funds withdrawn prior to age $59\frac{1}{2}$ are subject to a 10% penalty (except in the event of disability). Systematic withdrawals must be made by age $70\frac{1}{2}$ or be subject to a 50% tax. The minimum amount that must be withdrawn is based upon your life expectancy and the life expectancy of your designated beneficiary, if applicable.

How It Works

FACTUAL SITUATION

Sidney Gibson will retire in one year at age 65. He has IRA contributions which are in four different bank accounts. At retirement, Sidney will receive $50,000 in cash from his company's profit-sharing plan. He would like to have the IRA's and the company funds accumulate income until the maximum age of withdrawal ($70\frac{1}{2}$).

STEPS TO TAKE

1. Sidney should open an IRA Rollover Account with a securities firm and transfer the four existing IRA's into this account: The cash can then be invested in individual securities or mutual funds.

2. At retirement, he should roll over the company's funds ($50,000) into the IRA roll-over account and invest the proceeds into investments best suited to his specific needs. All income generated by the investments in Sidney's account will accumulate and compound tax free.

TAX TRAP FOR THE UNWARY

Under a law passed in July, 1992, if you choose to take your retirement plan assets (such as ESOP, profit sharing, or 401[k]) in hand, your employer *must* withhold 20% of your retirement plan distribution for taxes!

You can avoid the withholding simply by instructing your employer in writing to send your distribution *directly* to your IRA Rollover Account.

Annuities

What Is an Annuity?

It is a contract issued by an insurance company. This contract can be purchased with a lump sum payment or a series of periodic payments. In return, the insurance company guarantees the purchaser of the contract (called the annuitant) periodic payments of principal and interest for either the annuitant's lifetime or for a specified period of time. The withdrawal of interest only is also an option.

What Are the Benefits?

▶ *Safety*

Your principal and interest are guaranteed by a legal reserves insurance company. These types of insurance companies are required by law to establish reserves assuring the policyholder that the insurance company will have the assets which at least equal the future benefits provided by the policies.

▶ *Flexibility*

The annuitant decides when to take the income and therefore when to pay the taxes.

▶ *Interest accumulates on a tax-deferred basis*

No taxes are paid until funds are received. Interest rates are very competitive and are usually guaranteed for a specific period of time.

▶ *The contract is free from probate*

QUALIFIED PLANS (continued)

Types of Annuity Contracts

▶ *Single Premium Deferred Annuity*

Requires a single premium payment. Interest accumulates and compounds on a tax deferred basis.

▶ *Flexible Premium Annuity*

After the initial premium payment, future payments—at some minimum amount—may be added to the contract.

▶ *Single Premium Immediate Annuity*

An annuity contract purchased with a lump sum. The annuitant immediately begins to receive income—usually monthly—for a specified period of time or for life. A portion of the payment is considered a return of principal and therefore is not subject to taxation.

▶ *Variable Annuity*

May be purchased with a lump sum payment or a series of periodic payments. This type of annuity differs from the annuities enumerated above in only one aspect: Rather than receiving a guaranteed rate of return on your investment, your funds may be invested in a variety of investment vehicles such as Money Market Funds, stock or bond mutual funds, or U.S. Government Securities. At any given time, the total value of your annuity could be more or less than your original contribution, depending upon current market conditions. In the event of death, however, the beneficiary receives the original amount invested or the current value of the contract, whichever is greater. Therefore, the death benefit can never be less than the original amount invested.

Possible Uses for the Annuity Contract

1. Building a supplemental retirement plan.

2. Removing income from current taxation.

3. Maximizing those situations calling for the safest way to accumulate the most money with government approved tax advantages.

INSURANCE COMPANY RATINGS

The following organizations analyze and rate the financial stability of insurance companies:

A.M. Best Company

Duff & Phelps

Moody's

Standard & Poor's

You should ask your insurance agent or financial planner for the rating of each insurance company recommended to you.

TAX FACT

Withdrawals from a deferred annuity contract are subject to ordinary income taxation. Withdrawals prior to age 59 $\frac{1}{2}$ are subject to an additional 10% penalty.

INCOME ENHANCEMENT PROGRAM

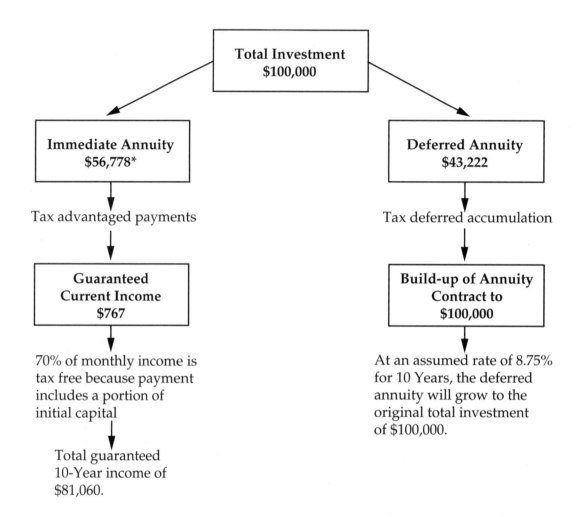

Total Investment
$100,000

Immediate Annuity
$56,778*

Deferred Annuity
$43,222

Tax advantaged payments

Tax deferred accumulation

Guaranteed
Current Income
$767

Build-up of Annuity
Contract to
$100,000

70% of monthly income is
tax free because payment
includes a portion of
initial capital

At an assumed rate of 8.75%
for 10 Years, the deferred
annuity will grow to the
original total investment
of $100,000.

Total guaranteed
10-Year income of
$81,060.

POINT TO PONDER

Had the original $100,000 been placed in a 10-year, 8% Certificate of
Deposit, the entire $80,000 of interest would have been taxed. How-
ever, only $24,300 is subject to taxation under the Income Enhance-
ment Program. Assuming a 28% federal tax bracket, the tax savings
would be $15,800 over the 10-year period. Less money to the govern-
ment, more money to you!

---

*Based upon a male age 55: A 10-year annuity contract is purchased—$100,000 was used
for illustration purposes. A lesser amount may of course be used.

INVESTMENT PORTFOLIO PLANNING

THREE POINTS TO KEEP IN MIND:

1) Identify your tolerance for risk.

2) Diversify your investments
   (also referred to as asset allocation).

3) Plan for the long term (ten years or longer).

64

THE INVESTMENT PYRAMID

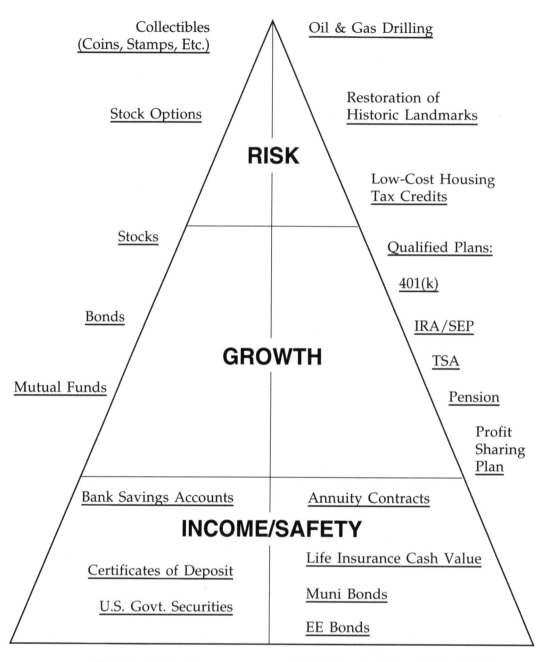

BUILD YOUR OWN PYRAMID

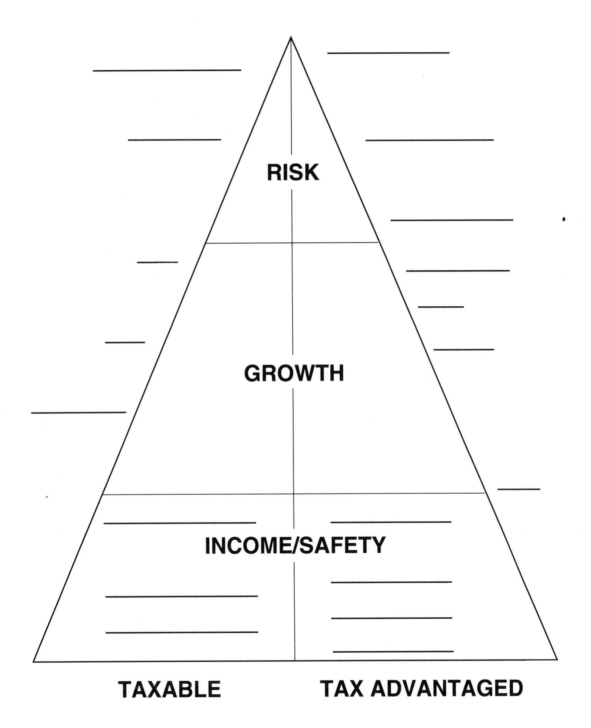

Use this page to fill in your investments. Do your investments reflect your goals and objectives?

SECTION

IV

Planning for the Future

COLLEGE FUNDING

If you have young children or plan to have children, the importance of long-term funding of college costs cannot be overstated. It may be appropriate for you to review the concept of dollar cost averaging on page 73, which provides for a long-term funding strategy. This concept emphasizes the importance of investing early and the compounding effect of money. You may also want to refer to the compound interest tables contained in Appendix B.

College costs have increased at a much higher rate than inflation for the past several years. Although the rate increase has slowed recently, college costs are still predicted to outpace inflation in the future. Financial aid for higher education, once a concern of low income families only, is now needed by almost everyone.

PLAN AHEAD FOR COLLEGE

COLLEGE FUNDING (continued)

Under present law, income earned in excess of $1,000 on (investment) funds held in the name of a child under age 14 will be taxed to the parents. The parents will pay the taxes on any excess income at their current income.

Example: Over the years John and Mary Smith have placed money in a savings account in the name of their 8 year old daughter, Tammy. Any interest earned on the account in excess of $1,000 must be reported by John and Mary on their tax return.

How to Avoid the Payment of Taxes in this Situation

There are two strategies that allow for the growth of the initial investment without incurring a tax. These are:

1. **Education IRA**—Created by the Taxpayer Relief Act of 1997. Features the withdrawal of earnings income tax-free. No deduction on initial contribution which is limited to $500 per year.

2. **Uniform Gift to Minors Act (UGMA)**—No limit on contributions made. This account is established with the child's Social Security number and either the parent or grandparent as custodian. Possible to avoid taxation on earnings until withdrawing for college purposes.

INFORMATION SOURCES ON COLLEGE COST AID

Colleges can be an invaluable source of information. Contact the college(s) you are most interested in directly.

There are also several helpful publications regarding college costs. Some of these sources include:

The Student Guide: Five Federal Financial Aid Programs (U.S. Government Printing Office, P.O. Box 37000, Washington, D.C. 20013). Describes all federal sources of financial aid in great detail and lists information sources for state aid for every state.

Applying for Financial Aid (American College Testing Program, P.O. Box 168, Iowa City, Iowa 52243).

The College Cost Book (College Entrance Examination Board, 45 Columbus Ave., New York, NY 10023). Available in most libraries and high school guidance counselor's offices.

Don't Miss Out, by Robert Leider (Octameron Press, P.O. Box 3437, Alexandria, VA 22302). Contains needs-analysis forms and advice.

The College Handbook (Peterson Guides, Inc., 166 Bunn Drive, P.O. Box 2123 Princeton, NJ 08450). Gives financial information on 1,700 U.S. colleges.

AUTHOR'S NOTE

You should discuss various funding plans with the colleges in which you are most interested. For example, you may be able to make a lump sum payment now (in the form of an annuity) and be guaranteed this sum of money will cover your child's college costs when he or she is old enough to begin college.

SYSTEMATIC INVESTING

WOULD YOU LIKE:

- An investment program for as little as $25 a month?

- A strategy designed to minimize risk of loss?

- A hedge against the uncertainties of the future?

- A method of systematically providing for future needs such as a college education for your children?

- A supplemental retirement plan?

THE NEXT PAGE MAY HELP CONVINCE YOU THAT A PLAN FOR SYSTEMATIC INVESTING IS A GOOD IDEA.

THE ADVANTAGES OF SYSTEMATIC INVESTING

Systematic investing can pay great rewards over a period of time. To illustrate, let's take a look at a technique called "dollar cost averaging."

Dollar cost averaging is simply the investment of a certain sum of money (usually in the same security or mutual fund) at regular intervals over a long period of time. It is basically an application of *time diversification* that enables investors to acquire more shares when the price is down and fewer shares when the price is up. Over time this reduces the average cost of the investment.

This program is particularly well suited for investors:

1. Who have the ability to invest a specific amount of money on a regular basis.

2. Who tend to follow a general investment policy of buying and holding.

3. Who generally do not want to try to forecast general economic trends.

The bar graph shown below illustrates the power of systematic investing (or dollar cost averaging) and the benefits of compounding over time.

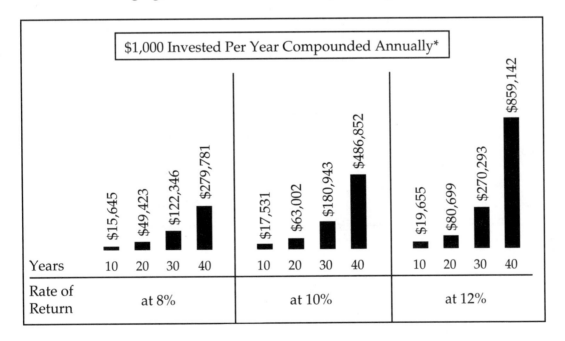

$1,000 Invested Per Year Compounded Annually*											
	$15,645	$49,423	$122,346	$279,781	$17,531	$63,002	$180,943	$486,852	$19,655	$80,699	$270,293	$859,142
Years	10	20	30	40	10	20	30	40	10	20	30	40
Rate of Return	at 8%				at 10%				at 12%			

*Assumes investments at the beginning of each year.

RETIREMENT PLANNING

Today's 50-year-olds can expect to live more than twenty years—approximately a third of their lives—in retirement.

Achieving financial security means accumulating a nest egg that will not only support you for two or three decades, but also resist the effects of inflation, taxation, or the possibility of failing health.

Successful retirement planning calls for astute investing, tax and estate planning, proper insurance management, and understanding social security and company sponsored pension benefits. Because it's your future, it's never too early to begin preparing for retirement.

There are five basic sources of retirement income:

1. Personal savings and investments

2. Employer sponsored retirement plans

3. Retirement plans for small business owners and the self-employed

4. The individual retirement account (IRA)

5. Social Security

> Retirement also calls for planning in other areas of a person's life, such as attitude, time-utilization, emotional and physical health, choice of housing, etc. For an outstanding book on retirement planning, send for *Comfort Zones: A Practical Guide for Retirement Planning* by Elwood Chapman using the information in the back of this book.

The assumption is often made that an individual's financial needs decrease after retirement. Although often true, this reduction in needs can be overstated. There is an increasing tendency for retired persons to not only live longer but also to lead more active lives. A growing number of retirees are choosing to remain active in civic, social, and recreational activities and are not significantly decreasing their standard of living.

Proper planning for retirement is more important than ever due to increasing life expectancy and the risk of "outliving one's income." Also, despite the assurances of politicians, there is no guarantee that social security will be available—especially in its current form—when you retire.

If you determine that your retirement objective—of a monthly income figure—falls short after you have completed the worksheet on page 77, one or more of the following variables will need to be changed or adjusted:

1. The amount you save or invest each year

2. The length of time until you retire

3. The annual growth rate on your investments

> **ARE YOU ADEQUATELY PREPARING FOR RETIREMENT? THE TIME TO START PLANNING IS NOW!**

RETIREMENT PLANNING QUESTIONNAIRE

The questions listed below will help you to begin thinking about your future if you have not already begun to do so. Answer each honestly.

1. How many years until you expect to retire?

   _____

2. What monthly income (net of taxes) will allow you to live comfortably?

   _____

3. Have you checked with the Social Security Administration to verify your contributions and monthly benefit?

   _____

4. Does your company have a pension plan? If so, record the amount of your monthly income at retirement.

   _____

5. Are you presently contributing the maximum amount allowable to a company sponsored retirement program? If so, how much?

   _____

6. If self-employed, are you contributing to a Keogh (pension/profit sharing plan)? If so, how much?

   _____

7. Have you been making annual contributions to an IRA?

   _____

8. Do you have a Long-Term Care Policy in the event of a prolonged nursing home stay?

   _____

9. What amount of income (after taxes) will your investments provide on a monthly basis?

   _____

10. Will you work part-time after retirement?

   _____

Now that you are in a "retirement" frame of mind, complete the exercise on the next page.

THE GOLDEN YEARS—WILL THEY GLITTER?

Retirement Goals

List those things you would like for a satisfying and fulfilling retirement. Consider where you want to live and what you want to do. Include travel and recreation in your plans. Don't worry about whether or not you can afford it now, just record what you really want. Use more paper if necessary.

Monthly Income and Expenses Worksheet

It's important to know your monthly financial needs both now and when you retire. You'll learn this by listing your average monthly income and expenses*. The difference between what you now earn and what you spend is important, because it represents the amount you will need to invest in your future. The table on page 113 will help you determine your income needs and expenses at retirement based on the inflation rate you select.

MONTHLY INCOME	NOW*	RETIREMENT
Salary (including spouse's)	$ _____	$ _____
Commissions, Bonuses, Tips	_____	_____
Interest, Dividends	_____	_____
Social Security	_____	_____
Pensions, Annuities, Trusts	_____	_____
Other	_____	_____
TOTAL INCOME (A)	$ _____	$ _____

MONTHLY INCOME	NOW*	RETIREMENT
Housing (mortgage payments/rent)	$ _____	$ _____
Maintenance & Repairs	_____	_____
Utilities	_____	_____
Loan payments (car, personal)	_____	_____
Food	_____	_____
Clothing	_____	_____
Transportation	_____	_____
Medical (health) expenses	_____	_____
Insurance premiums	_____	_____
Recreational/travel	_____	_____
Charitable contributions	_____	_____
Taxes—property, income	_____	_____
Other	_____	_____
TOTAL EXPENSES (B)	$ _____	$ _____
A – B = SURPLUS (OR DEFICIT)	$ _____	$ _____

*Your current figures can be obtained from the Income (or Cash Flow) Statement that you previously completed on page 19.

RETIREMENT PLANNING EXERCISE

What have you learned? Will your income at retirement be sufficient to meet your expenditures? If not, what adjustments can you begin to make to correct the situation? In the space below, list those action items which will be necessary to meet your retirement objectives. For example, save more each month, reduce outstanding debt, plan to work 10 hours per week (even when officially retired), cut back on your retirement expectations, delay the age of your retirement, etc.

_____

_____

_____

_____

_____

_____

_____

_____

_____

_____

_____

_____

_____

_____

_____

SOCIAL SECURITY AND MEDICARE

Questions on Social Security

Q. *How old must I be to qualify for Social Security?*

A. You must be at least sixty-two.

Q. *When and where should I file for Social Security benefits?*

A. Three months before you plan to retire. Apply at your local Social Security Administration office.

Q. *Does the Social Security Administration require any special papers when I file?*

A. Yes. Bring your Social Security card, a copy of your birth or baptismal certificate, and a copy of your last withholding income tax statement or Federal income tax return.

Q. *How do I qualify for benefits?*

A. You receive credit for a certain amount of work. Work credits are figured in "quarters of coverage." You get one quarter of coverage if your wages come to at least $540 in a quarter of a year. To be "fully insured"—that is, to be guaranteed full retirement benefits—you need 33 quarters if you reach 62 in 1984, 34 quarters if you reach age 62 in 1985. The maximum requirement is now 40 quarters (10 years) for those reaching age 62 in 1992 or later.

Q. *How much will I get?*

A. This varies from person to person, depending on individual factors (such as the number of years you worked, your average yearly earnings, your age at retirement, etc.). Your Social Security office will figure it out for you after you apply. Currently, the maximum monthly benefit for a retired worker at age 65 is over $1000. (Benefits may begin as early as age 62 at a lesser amount.)

SOCIAL SECURITY AND MEDICARE
(continued)

Q. *How much can I earn and still get my full Social Security retirement check?*

A. The 1996 limits on annual earnings are $8,280 for those under age 65 and 64 and $11,520 for those between the ages of 65 and 70. There are no limits for those 70 and older.

Social Security checks will be reduced by $1.00 in benefits for each $2.00 earned over the maximum allowed for those 62 and 64 in age. Between the ages of 65 and 69, the reduction is $1.00 for each $3.00 earned over the maximum.

Unearned income such as interest, stock dividends, and income from rental property will not affect Social Security payments.

Medicare Health Insurance Information

Medicare is a federal health insurance program for people age 65 and older. It also covers some people under 65 who are disabled. You must enroll to receive Medicare coverage. The initial enrollment period for medicare begins 3 months before you reach age 65 and lasts for 7 months. You must apply at your local Social Security Administration office during the 7 month period in order to receive Medicare coverage when you first become eligible.

Medicare has two parts: (A) Hospital Insurance and (B) Medical Insurance. The basic hospital insurance plan will pay for most of the costs related to hospitalization as well as certain related care when you leave the hospital. The medical insurance plan pays for a large part of your doctor bills plus other medical expenses not covered by the basic hospital insurance plan.

There is no monthly cost to you for Hospital Insurance, but you must pay a monthly premium for Medical Insurance which is normally deducted from your Social Security check.

ESTATE PLANNING

Estate planning, at its simplest, involves the preservation and distribution of wealth, either before or after death.

Proper estate planning can help to:

- Alleviate administrative court costs

- Provide for orderly distribution of assets without delay

- Minimize legal fees and estate taxes

Despite the necessity for, and advantage of, early planning to divide one's estate, most people are reluctant to deal with the subject. A financial planner can review your estate situation and then direct you to an attorney who specializes in this particular field of law. A financial planner can "nudge" you to do what you know should be done.

> ONCE AGAIN, THE OBJECTIVE IS
> TO EXAMINE AND DIAGNOSE YOUR
> NEEDS IN THIS VERY CRITICAL AREA.

ESTATE PLANNING IS A MUST

PERSONAL ESTATE PLAN ANALYSIS

This short exercise will help you think about your estate and determine what provisions may be needed to preserve your wealth for the benefit of your survivors.*

	Yes	No	I Don't Know
Do I have a will?	❏	❏	❏
Has my will been revised during the last three years to adjust for any significant changes in my personal/ financial situation or estate tax legislation?	❏	❏	❏
Do I understand the different tax ramifications of holding title to my assets—i.e., joint tenancy vs. community property.	❏	❏	❏
Have I considered any special considerations my survivors might have? (example: handicaps, personalities, abilities)	❏	❏	❏
Are there any special tax planning provisions (such as a trust) in my estate plan?	❏	❏	❏
Will my estate provide enough liquidity to meet immediate family needs and pay all outstanding debts?	❏	❏	❏
Do my heirs/executor know where to locate my important papers and documents?*	❏	❏	❏
Upon my death, will my children's interests be protected in the event my spouse remarries?	❏	❏	❏
Have I recently reviewed the beneficiary designation of my life insurance policies, IRAs and company retirement plans to determine if any changes might be appropriate?	❏	❏	❏

If you have *not* answered yes to at least five of the questions, it indicates a lack of attention to this area of your financial affairs. Meeting with a financial planner or estate planning attorney would be advisable.

---

*Before answering, please refer to Appendix A regarding the location of your personal financial records. If you have not collected this information, now would be an excellent time to do so using the forms provided.

Why a Will Is Important

Several reasons. First, Uncle Sam gets more if you die intestate (without a will). Also, there are delays, higher court costs, and the involvement of state appointed administrators (strangers) to settle your personal affairs if you do not have a will.

What a Will Can Do

If you die testate (with a will), your assets will be distributed according to the terms of the will. Your personal wishes and instructions will be carried out.

ADDITIONAL METHODS OF TRANSFERRING ASSETS TO AN HEIR:

Gift—i.e., giving property away outright; $10,000 per year per person without incurring any tax consequences for the "giver."

Title—i.e., Joint tenancy with the right of survivorship (JT/WROS). For example: property titled John Doe and Mary Doe as Joint Tenants will pass to the survivor of these two regardless of what the will might state.

Contract—i.e., naming someone as the beneficiary in a life insurance policy. At the time of death of the insured, the named beneficiary will receive the designated amount directly from the insurance company free of income taxes.

Trust*—a separate legal entity created for (1) tax planning or estate tax reduction, (2) eliminating probate costs and delays, (3) family planning—determining when and how much to distribute.

The above methods should be thoughtfully coordinated (with the help of an estate planning attorney) to maximize the financial benefits to those for whom you wish to provide. Your estate plan should be reviewed every two or three years to make adjustments for changes in tax laws or your personal/financial situation.

---

*See page 85 for a discussion of a living trust.

DO-IT-YOURSELF FEDERAL ESTATE TAX CALCULATOR

A. Amount of taxable estate $_____

B. Aggregate of all post-1976 *adjusted taxable gifts*   +_____

C. Sum of "A" and "B" $_____

D. Tentative estate tax on "C" (from current tax table) $_____

E. Aggregate of all gift taxes paid on post-1976 gifts   −_____

F. Tentative estate tax on ("D" less "E") $_____

G. Estate tax credit (if any)   −_____

H. State death tax credit and any other credits (if applicable)   −_____

I. Estate tax payable ("F" less "G" and "H" but not less than $0) $_____

AUTHOR'S NOTE

- Beginning 1998, taxable estates under $625,000 pay no federal estate tax. By the year 2006, the transfer tax exemption will be $1,000,000.

- Some states have an Inheritance Tax. Contact an estate planning attorney for specifics in your state.

THE LIVING TRUST: A VERSATILE ESTATE PLANNING TOOL

What It Is

An arrangement whereby you (as Trustor) transfer legal ownership of your property to yourself as Trustee. For example: John and Mary Thomas would transfer title to their house from "John and Mary Thomas as joint tenants" to "John and Mary Thomas, Trustees of the Thomas Family Trust."

How to Establish

The trust document must be prepared by an attorney. It is a flexible arrangement that costs you, as Trustee, virtually nothing to administer during your lifetime. The living trust (also known as an Inter Vivos Trust) may be amended or revoked (terminated) while you, and your spouse, if married are alive. When either spouse dies, the trust document becomes irrevocable.

Benefits*

- It provides privacy—the trust document does not become a part of the public record.

- It avoids probate and unnecessary delays in settling your estate.

- It can eliminate the payment of income taxes on highly appreciated property.

- It can be structured to provide professional management of the assets for the surviving spouse, if he/she has little investment or business experience.

- It provides for a conservatorship in the event of physical or mental incapacitation.

- It can save your estate money by reducing estate taxes at the second death.

- It reduces chances of having your estate contested by a disgruntled heir. The establishment of a trust shows clear intent on your part.

- Finally, it is a valuable planning tool to benefit those with moderate-size estates to very large estates.

The above is one major type of trust. Be aware there are many different types of trusts available to meet your specific objectives. Consult an estate planning specialist for specific trust(s) that may be appropriate for you.

---

*The total number of benefits will vary according to your particular circumstances.

PLANNED GIVING ARRANGEMENTS

Charity Begins at Home

How would you like to:

1. Generate an income tax deduction.

2. Increase and diversify your income.

3. Avoid the payment of a capital gains tax on highly appreciated/low yielding assets (typically stocks or real estate).

4. Eliminate asset management problems.

5. Reduce estate taxes.

6. Avoid probate costs.

7. Assist your favorite charity.

These benefits can be obtained by contributing a currently owned asset to a charitable organization.

AUTHOR'S NOTE

The area of charitable giving is very personal and can be quite complex and sophisticated. For these reasons, it is advisable to consult with professional advisors. You may want to start by contacting your favorite charity.

SECTION

V

Case Studies

AUTHOR'S NOTES

The purpose of the following four case studies (client situations) is to let you practice your working knowledge of the terms, concepts and principles covered in this book. You can practice prescribing specific courses of action. There are no absolutely correct answers.

Everyone's siutation should be reviewed annually to adjust for significant changes in personal or financial circumstances or tax laws. This annual review stresses the importance of monitoring, which is essential to the financial planning process.

The road to success is paved with good intentions, sound investments *and* proper planning.

MAXIMIZING INVESTMENT RETURNS

Personal Information

Tom Wilton, age 51
Senior engineer with an aerospace firm
Annual income $75,000
Mary Wilton, age 48
Housewife
Two grown children
Have lived in same home for 21 years
Both have a moderate tolerance for risk

Financial Information

$30,000—in various savings and money market accounts; average yield
   of 5%.
$12,000 in several underperforming stocks.
A 20-year-old $10,000 insurance contract containing $5,000 in cash values;
   annual cash value build-up is 4.5%.
A $100,000 company sponsored group term insurance policy.
$650 in monthly surplus, which is added to savings.

Goals and Objectives

Generate a higher yield on investments but take only moderate risk
   to do so.
Maintain an emergency fund of at least $10,000.

YOUR RECOMMENDATIONS

- _____

- _____

- _____

Compare your recommendations with the author's recommendations on the
next page.

MAXIMIZING INVESTMENT RETURNS
(continued)

Author's Suggested Recommendations

Observations

The Wiltons presently have no capital growth potential and little protection from taxation.

Recommendations

Surrender the life insurance policy for the $5,000 in cash values and sell the individual stocks. Add $20,000 in savings for a total of $37,000 and invest this amount in a variable annuity contract for long term growth and income.

Invest $200 of the $650 monthly surplus in a balanced (combination stocks and bonds) mutual fund. This sytematic investment approach takes advantage of dollar cost averaging.

Put half of remaining current savings/money market accounts ($5,000) into a tax-free money market fund in order to generate a higher net (after tax) return. Leave remaining half of reserves ($5,000) in the savings account.

Results

The variable annuity contract will provide a greater growth potential than either the life insurance cash values or the stocks. Earnings will accumulate and compound tax-free until withdrawn and can be earmarked to supplement retirement income.

The monthly mutual fund investment program represents a conservative approach to long-term investing (dollar cost averaging) and a hedge against inflation.

HELPING THE SINGLE PARENT THRIVE

CASE STUDY #2

Personal Information

Pamela Atkins, age 39
Office Administrator for a small software firm that does not have a
  retirement plan in force
Annual salary $24,000
Recently divorced—lives with 15 yr. old daughter, Diane
Ex-husband provides $700 per month in child support. He also maintains
  a $50,000 life insurance policy naming Pam as the beneficiary.

Financial Information

Pamela and Diane currently live in an apartment renting for $850
  per month.
When former residence (owned with ex-husband) is sold, Pamela will
  receive $38,000 in cash (after taxes).
Has $2,500 in savings, $5,000 in credit card debt (18% annual interest
  rate); maximum monthly payments on credit cards are $250.
Pamela recently received an inheritance of $17,000 from her father's
  estate that she placed in a 90 day Certificate of Deposit.
Pamela has never attempted to budget her income or expenses.

Goals and Objectives

Feel comfortable and in control of current financial situation.
Purchase a $90,000 condominium.
Build a reserve for the future (retirement fund).

YOUR RECOMMENDATIONS

- _____

- _____

- _____

Compare your recommendations with the author's recommendations on the
next page.

HELPING THE SINGLE PARENT THRIVE (continued)

Author's Suggested Recommendations

Observations

Short-term debt (credit cards) has a negative impact on monthly cash flow.

Must control finances through diligent use of a budget (income and expense forecasting).

Recommendations

Develop a monthly Income (or cash flow) Statement and create a monthly Budget. Monitor both on a regular basis. Attempt to develop a monthly surplus to add to the savings account.

Once an amount equal to three months fixed living expenses (estimated at $5,000) has been reached in the savings account, use the cash surplus to fund a monthly investment program (dollar cost averaging) in a growth mutual fund.

Use $5,000 of the inheritance money to pay off all credit card debt (18% interest) when the CD matures in 90 days.

Use proceeds from sale of previous home and $2,000 of the inheritance funds to make a $40,000 downpayment on a $90,000 condominium. Monthly payments (estimated at $800 including property taxes) consist largely of tax deductible interest, thereby generating a tax savings of $200 per month. The remainder of the inheritance ($10,000) can be used to upgrade and furnish the condominium.

Of the $200 per month in tax savings, $166 can be used to invest in an IRA, which will generate another $2,000 tax deduction for the year.

Results

Creation of the Income Statement and Budget will help Pam monitor her cash flow on a more consistent basis and give her a feeling of being in better control of her finances.

Elimination of credit card debt and use of the monthly surplus for savings (initially) and then investing, will help build financial security for the future.

Purchase of a condominium will create a tax write-off through interest and property tax deductions. The IRA will also create a tax write-off while building a retirement fund for the future.

ADDING GLITTER TO THE GOLDEN YEARS

CASE STUDY #3

Personal Information

Harold Smith, age 64
Senior Manager for a public utilities company
Annual salary $57,000
Betty Smith, age 57
Housewife. Has no interest in financial matters. Harold has always
managed their money.
Harold will retire in one year at age 65
Neither has a will at the present time
Have 4 grown children, all of whom are married
Own a four unit apartment building

Financial Information

Estimated gross monthly income needed at retirement—$3,000
Projected sources of monthly retirement income:

company pension plan	$1,700
Social Security	$ 800
rental income (fourplex)	$ 400
Total	$2,900

Estimated vested benefits from company salary savings program at age
65 is $125,000. An estimate of the annual income that can be gener-
ated from this source has *not* been included in the projected sources
of monthly retirement income.
$20,000 in a Certificate of Deposit maturing in one year.
Harold has an IRA with the company credit union (total value $15,000).

Goals and Objectives

Maximize income to provide for a comfortable retirement.
At retirement, stay ahead of inflation without depleting investment
principal.
Simplify the tracking and administration of all investments at retirement.
Provide for the efficient and orderly disposition of assets in the event of
either spouse's death.

ADDING GLITTER TO THE GOLDEN YEARS (continued)

YOUR RECOMMENDATIONS

- _____

- _____

- _____

Compare your recommendations with the author's recommendations on the next page.

Author's Suggested Recommendations

Observations

The Smiths live within their means and should enjoy a comfortable retirement.

Recommendations

When the $20,000 Certificate of Deposit matures, place the $10,000 into an insured Money Market Account to serve as an emergency fund. Place the remaining $10,000 in a single premium deferred annuity contract.

Establish an IRA Rollover Account. Transfer the existing IRA currently in the credit union to this new account. Invest the funds in a balanced Mutual Fund that will provide growth as well as income.

At retirement, transfer the vested company retirement funds ($125,000) into the IRA Rollover Account and place the money in a portfolio of Mutual Funds. Harold can make withdrawals from this account at any time to supplement his monthly retirement income. There are no income taxes to pay until funds are withdrawn from the Rollover Account.

See an estate planning attorney to draft an estate plan designed to meet the needs of both Harold and Betty. Placing their assets in an Inter Vivos (living) Trust with a provision for professional management will be of great benefit to Betty if Harold predeceases her.

Results

The retirement funds placed in the IRA Rollover Account will accumulate and compound tax free. Any additional monthly income needed may be withdrawn from the account and will be subject to ordinary taxation.

The establishment of a $10,000 money market account will provide the Smiths with an emergency source of funds equal to approximately three times their fixed living expenses ($3,000 × 3 mos. = $9,000).

The interest on the annuity contract is taxed only if withdrawn. A good tax deferral investment.

Drafting an estate plan will provide for the orderly disposition of their assets and provide Betty with the protection and investment advice that she needs.

PROVIDING FOR THE FUTURE

CASE STUDY #4

Personal Information

Ron Woodman, age 45
Sales representative for a manufacturing firm
Annual salary $40,000
Janice Woodman, age 40
Bank loan officer
Annual salary $35,000
Have two children, ages 6 and 9

Financial Information

Annual amount available for investing or savings—$4,500
Ron is currently contributing 3% (6% is allowable) to his company's
    401(k) plan
A college fund has been established for the children by the grandparents
Have mutual funds valued at $25,000
Have $10,000 in a bank passbook account

Goals and Objectives

Provide greater insurance protection for Janice and the children
Earmark funds for college expenses
Build a reserve to supplement future retirement income

YOUR RECOMMENDATIONS

- _____

- _____

- _____

Compare your recommendations with the author's recommendations on the next page.

Author's Suggested Recommendations

Observations

> The Woodmans are very disciplined financially as evidenced by their annual surplus of $4,500.
> Contributions made by the grandparents will greatly help to reduce college costs.

Recommendations

> Use $2,250 of the annual surplus to purchase a $160,000 insurance policy with a seven year vanishing premium. The estimated cash value at 65 would be $36,153.
> Use the balance of the disposable income ($2,250) to increase Ron's contributions to his 401(k) contribution to a maximum of 6% of salary. All contributions are exempt from taxation. No taxes are paid until withdrawals begin at retirement.
> Earmark stocks and mutual funds to supplement future college expenses.
> Transfer the funds in the bank passbook account to an insured Money Market Account.

Results

> The insurance policy will provide a tax free death benefit and a cash value of $36,153 at age 65. Ron could, at that time, borrow out of the contract on a tax-free basis approximately $2,000 per year (for more than 20 years) to supplement his retirement income.
> Using the securities to supplement college costs will avoid the necessity to use current income, which can continue to be invested in the company 401(k) plan.
> The insured Money Market Account will provide a higher yield than the passbook account with commensurate safety.

SECTION

VI

Monitor the Results

THE FINANCIAL FITNESS EXAM

The following exam will help you determine your basic understanding of the material presented in this book.

	True	False
1. Personal financial planning goals should be general in nature.	❏	❏
2. Life insurance payments to a named beneficiary are taxable as ordinary income.	❏	❏
3. A living (Inter Vivos) trust will benefit those with modest estates as well as those with very large estates.	❏	❏
4. An income (or cash flow) statement lists all of your assets and liabilities.	❏	❏
5. Current tax law allows for the deduction of state and local income taxes and real estate (property) taxes against ordinary income.	❏	❏
6. Keeping secret the whereabouts of personal papers will provide for greater family security.	❏	❏
7. Both municipal and corporate bonds generate tax-free income.	❏	❏
8. The income earned on an IRA must be reported as taxable income each year.	❏	❏
9. School district or nonprofit organization employees may contribute to a tax sheltered annuity (TSA).	❏	❏

THE FINANCIAL FITNESS EXAM (continued)

	True	False
10. Married people usually die intestate.	❏	❏
11. The longer the maturity date, the greater the appreciation on a bank Certificate of Deposit.	❏	❏
12. Diversification is a sound defensive strategy toward investing.	❏	❏
13. Dollar cost averaging is well suited for short-term needs such as your next vacation.	❏	❏
14. Anyone over age 30 could benefit from long-term planning.	❏	❏
15. Mortgage interest deductions on first and second homes are limited to the sum total of the price you originally paid for the house plus the cost of home (capital) improvements.	❏	❏
16. The interest on consumer debt (such as credit cards) continues to be a viable tax-deductible item.	❏	❏
17. There are insurance products that generate tax-free income.	❏	❏
18. Your tax bracket is not important in computing the after-tax yield on an investment.	❏	❏
19. A young married couple with a small income should invest discretionary funds in municipal bonds.	❏	❏
20. A budget is used to forecast income and expenses.	❏	❏

ANSWERS TO THE EXAM

Grading Key

Number correct

16–20   You're on the way to "financial fitness".

10–15   It's time to schedule a routine check-up. Review the sections you found most difficult.

Less than 10   Take two aspirin, read the book again, and call a financial planner in the morning!

1. *F.* Goals should be specific—use dollar figures and dates.

2. *F.* Proceeds to a named beneficiary are received income tax free.

3. *T.* A living (Inter Vivos) trust is a versatile estate planning tool that offers both tax and nontax benefits.

4. *F.* A *balance sheet* lists your assets and liabilities. The *income statement* lists your income and expenses.

5. *T.* These provisions remain unaffected by the 1986 Tax Reform Act.

6. *F.* Key advisors, family members and your executor/executrix should know the location of all important financial information.

7. *F.* Only a municipal bond will generate tax-free income.

8. *F.* Income accumulates and compounds tax free. Only when funds are withdrawn are they subject to taxation.

9. *T.*

10. *F.* The term "intestate" means to die without a will.

11. *F.* The original deposit does not appreciate in value. It generates taxable income.

12. *T.*

13. *F.* It is better suited to long-term needs such as college funding or retirement.

14. *T.* It's never too early to prepare for the future.

15. *T.* However, this sum may be exceeded if you borrow against your home for qualified educational or medical expenses.

16. *F.* Interest on consumer debt is no longer a tax-deductible item.

17. *T.* It is possible to borrow the accumulated cash values in a Whole Life or Universal Life Contract and thereby avoid paying income taxes.

18. *F.* Your tax bracket has a direct effect (See page 84).

19. *F.* Growth of capital is more important than tax exempt income in a low tax bracket.

20. *T.* A budget looks at your future plan for earning and spending money.

GLOSSARY

Annuity—A contract purchased from an insurance company. Interest is paid on the principal amount and accumulates tax free. Withdrawals are subject to taxation. Annuities are often used for retirement planning.

Appreciation—Increase in the dollar value of an asset (such as a share of stock) over time.

Beneficiary—A person named to receive the income or property from a trust or life insurance policy.

Bond—A debt instrument (liability) with a specified interest rate and maturity date. Issued by the government (federal, state, local) and agencies of the federal government and/or corporations.

Certificate of Deposit (C.D.)—A time deposit with a specified maturity date.

Common Stock—A security representing ownership in a corporation.

Community Property—Property that either or both spouses acquire during marriage. Each spouse has an undivided half interest in their community property. Upon death, each spouse can dispose of only his or her half of the community property by will. This form of property ownership is limited to a few states.

Estate—The total amount of assets and liabilities belonging to a person at the time of his/her death.

Executor/Executrix—The personal representative appointed in a will to settle an estate. It can be either a person or a corporate entity such as a bank or trust company.

Guardian/Conservator—A person appointed by the court to take care of the needs of a minor, incapacitated or incompetent person (the ward). The guardian's duty to care for the ward's needs continues until the ward reaches the age of majority, or once again, becomes competent.

Heir—One receiving a person's property (inheritance) either by will or law.

Inflation—The loss of purchasing power due to a general rise in prices (goods and services).

Investment Capital—Original amount invested.

Joint Tenancy—The co-ownership of property by two or more persons related or unrelated. Upon death of a co-owner, the surviving owner(s) automatically receive(s) the deceased's share. No probate is involved.

Leverage—A magnification of the potential return (appreciation) on an investment. Often accomplished by controlling an asset with a relatively small amount of invested capital.

Limited Partnership—A syndication of investors (limited partners) who invest funds on a joint basis with a managing general partner. Investor's liability is limited to his/her original capital contribution.

Life Insurance Cash Values—The build-up of cash on an annual basis inside of a permanent (whole life, interest sensitive, or universal) life policy.

Living Will—An expression of an individual's wish that when faced with imminent death, sophisticated, life-sustaining medical technology should not be used to prolong life. This declaration should be kept separate from a person's legal will.

Money Market Account—A savings account that pays a money market (short-term securities) rate of interest.

Municipal Bond—A debt obligation issued by a state or local government agency. Income generated by such bonds is exempt from federal (and often state) income taxes.

Mutual Fund—A professionally managed open-end investment company. The three major categories of funds are income, growth, and balanced (a combination of income and growth).

Preferred Stock—Noted for paying a fixed dividend. In the event of a corporate liquidation, holder of such stock would be paid before all common stock holders.

Probate—The process by which a court determines legal title to property following a death. Probate can be costly and time consuming.

Real Estate Investment Trust (R.E.I.T.)—Ownership of shares in a portfolio of real estate properties or mortgage investments. At least 90% of the income passes through to the shareholders. Shares can be readily liquidated in the stock market.

GLOSSARY (continued)

Trust—An arrangement in which one party (Trustee) holds legal title to property for the benefit of another (Beneficiary). Often used to avoid probate and reduce estate taxes.

U.S. Government Securities Fund—A professionally managed portfolio of debt obligations (bills, bonds, notes) issued or guaranteed by the U.S. Government. Seeks high level of current income consistent with safety of principal. Similar to a mutual fund in structure.

U.S. Savings Bond—Guaranteed by the federal government. Purchased at a 50% discount from face value. Issued in face amounts from $50 to $10,000. No taxes to pay on accumulated interest until the bond is redeemed.

Will—A validly executed document that disposes of an individual's property and other owned interests when he/she dies.

RESOURCES

Protect yourself and your family from future financial hardship by educating yourself now. Learn as much as you can about your retirement years. Write to the resources below to get more information.

Consumer Information Center
Pueblo, CO 81009

> For catalog of free and low-cost government publications.

American Association of Retired Persons
1090 K Street, NW
Washington, DC 20044

> Private organization that provides help and support for retirees.

Social Security Administration
6401 Security Boulevard
Baltimore, MD 21235

> To receive a free statement of earnings credited to your Social Security record, call your nearest Social Security office for more information.

Administration on Aging
c/o Department of Health and Human Services
330 Independence Avenue, SW
Washington, DC 20201

> Free booklets on services for the elderly.

Veterans Administration
810 Vermont Avenue, NW
Washington, DC 20201

> Provides a variety of services for qualified veterans.

HOW TO CHOOSE A FINANCIAL PLANNER

AUTHOR'S NOTE

Many financial planners do not charge for the initial one hour consultation. The objective of this initial meeting is to learn about each other. Bring information to your first meeting such as a balance sheet, last year's tax return, estate plan documents, insurance policies and retirement plan benefits. Be prepared to discuss your situation in specific terms.

You and the planner should be compatible. This is often determined by his/her investment philosophy as compared to your own. Also you should feel a high level of trust (just as with your personal physician). You should feel confident and comfortable with your planner. The following checklist should help you to evaluate and select a financial planning professional:

QUESTIONS TO ASK AND POINTS TO CONSIDER:

1. Ask to see a sample of the planner's work, such as an investment analysis or financial plan. The planner should provide concrete evidence of his/her competence and ability to deal with a vast array of financial situations.

2. Ask what type of clientele the planner works with. It is common for planners to work within particular professional groups, income levels and/or age groups.

3. Request a disclosure statement that provides details of the planner's education, background, number of years experience, and areas of specialization. The size of the firm is not as important as the qualifications of the planner.

4. Ask the planner to provide the names of clients who you may contact regarding the quality of service rendered.

5. Ask to see credentials. Industry credentials such as Certified Financial Planner (CFP) and membership in the Registry of Financial Planning Practitioners (established by the IAFP) indicate a commitment to excellence. Either of these credentials identify practitioners with the education, experience and ethics considered necessary to perform their services professionally.

To become a CFP, an individual must pass a six-part curriculum and have a minimum of three years of full-time experience of direct client contact.

The standards for the Registry of Financial Planning Practitioners have been established by the IAFP and help the public identify financial planning practitioners who meet the standards essential to the practice of total financial planning. To be a Registry member, an individual must hold certain approved designations, certifications, or degrees and have a minimum of three years experience practicing total financial planning.

6. Inquire if the planner is a member in good standing of the International Association for Financial Planning (IAFP) and the Institute of Certified Financial Planners (ICFP).

- IAFP—has a broad-based membership that comes from many related disciplines: financial planners, accountants, attorneys, bankers, trust officers, representatives of the insurance, real estate and securities field, and suppliers of various financial products and services.

- ICFP—only Certified Financial Planners can be members.

7. Discuss the planner's method of compensation, which may be:

- *Fees*—Either an hourly rate or a flat charge for a specific period of time (such as one year). Fees are usually determined on a case-by-case basis.

- *Commissions*—Generated from investment products placed through the planner.

- *Fees and Commissions*—Those planners who are Registered Investment Advisors (RIA) may charge a fee as well as receive commissions.

8. Ask questions. Learn as much as you can about the planner. This can initially be accomplished both by phone and during the introductory meeting.

HOW TO CONTACT A FINANCIAL ADVISOR

► Through a friend or associate currently working with an advisor who is satisfied with the results.

► Through a national organization such as those listed below; who will provide referrals in your area:

ICFP—Institute of Certified Financial Planners
7600 East Eastman, Ste. 301, Denver, CO 80231-4397
(303) 759-4900

IAFP—International Association for Financial Planning
5775 Glenridge Drive N.E., Ste. B300, Atlanta, GA 30328
(404) 845-0011

Registry of Financial Planning Practitioners
Two Concourse Parkway, Ste. 800, Atlanta, GA 30328
(404) 845-0011

► Via free public seminars. Many financial planners, accountants, and attorneys conduct informational seminars that could be of interest to you. Consult your local newspaper for announcements.

► Through the yellow pages. (Sometimes the best planners don't advertise their services.)

► Through courses offered by your local community college or adult education program.

AUTHOR'S NOTE

In addition to the services offered by independent financial planners, you may wish to explore the services offered by the financial planning departments of various banks, insurance companies, and stock brokerage firms. In all cases, the same questions should be asked.

APPENDIX A

RECORD OF IMPORTANT
FINANCIAL INFORMATION

Checking account   (No. _____)   (No. _____)

Located at: _____   _____

_____   _____

Savings account   (No. _____)   (No. _____)

Located at: _____   _____

_____   _____

Other—(Credit Union, Certificate of Deposit, etc.)

(No. _____)   (No. _____)

Located at: _____   _____

_____   _____

Key Advisors:	Name	Addresses	Telephone
Attorney	_____	_____	_____
Accountant	_____	_____	_____
Financial Planner	_____	_____	_____
Banker	_____	_____	_____
Insurance Agent	_____	_____	_____
Stock Broker	_____	_____	_____
Other	_____	_____	_____
Other	_____	_____	_____

(This page may be reproduced without further permission)

RECORD OF IMPORTANT FINANCIAL INFORMATION (continued)

Safety Deposit Box (SDB) No. _____

Located at: _____

Keys to box are located at: _____

Location of important documents and papers: Check one

	Home	Office	Safety Deposit Box
Wills/Trusts	❏	❏	❏
Deed to property	❏	❏	❏
Life insurance policies	❏	❏	❏
Birth certificate	❏	❏	❏
Stock/bond certificates	❏	❏	❏
Investment papers (such as limited partnership certificates)	❏	❏	❏
Auto Registration (Pink Slip)	❏	❏	❏
IRA paperwork	❏	❏	❏
Business Agreements	❏	❏	❏
Company retirement benefits	❏	❏	❏
Other (list)			
_____	❏	❏	❏
_____	❏	❏	❏

The executor of your will should have a copy of this information in order to help facilitate the settlement of your estate.

(This page may be reproduced without further permission)

APPENDIX B

COMPOUND INTEREST TABLES

ONE DOLLAR LEFT ON DEPOSIT				
Year	6%	8%	10%	12%
1	1.06	1.08	1.10	1.12
5	1.34	1.47	1.61	1.76
10	1.79	2.16	2.59	3.10
15	2.40	3.17	4.18	5.47
20	3.21	4.66	6.73	9.65
25	4.29	6.85	10.83	17.00
30	5.74	10.06	17.45	29.96

EXAMPLE: One dollar left on deposit for 10 years at 8% will grow to $2.16.

Go down the year column to the 10th year. Then come over to the 8% column to get the figure of 2.16. Then $1.00 × 2.16 = $2.16.

ONE DOLLAR DEPOSITED AT THE END OF EACH YEAR				
Year	6%	8%	10%	12%
1	1.06	1.08	1.10	1.12
5	1.34	1.47	1.61	1.76
10	1.79	2.16	2.59	3.10
15	2.40	3.17	4.18	5.47
20	3.21	4.66	6.73	9.65
25	4.29	6.85	10.83	17.00
30	5.74	10.06	17.45	29.96

ONE DOLLAR DEPOSITED EACH YEAR

EXAMPLE: One dollar deposited at the end of each year for 15 years earning 10% will grow to a total of $31.77.

Go down the year column to the 15th year. Then come over to the 10% column to get the figure of 31.77. Then $1.00 × 31.77 = $31.77.

APPENDIX C

TAXPAYER RELIEF ACT OF 1997

The Taxpayer Relief Act of 1997 is now law and the news could bode well for many investors. The following are some of the highlights from the tax bill.

- Reduction in capital gains tax to top rate of 20% (holding restrictions apply).

- The first $250,000 (if single), $500,000 (if married, filing jointly) in capital gains on a home sold on or after May 7, 1997 is excluded from taxes.

  In addition, this break is available to homeowners at any age and an entirely new exemption may be possible every two years.

- Gradual increase in the unified credit (relating to assets exempt from estate tax) from $600,000 to $1M in 2006.

- Elimination of 15% "success" tax on large retirement plan distributions, both to the individual and his/her estate retroactive to 1/1/97.

- Expansion of deductibility thresholds for traditional IRAs. Starting in 1998, Active Participants (covered by employer-sponsored plan) can make fully deductible contributions if the AGI is $30,000 or less for singles or $50,000 or less if married.

  Partial deductions allowed if singles AGI is between $30,000–$40,000 and for marrieds if AGI is between $50,000–$60,.000.

  Thresholds will increase annually until 2007 when thresholds will begin at $60,000 for singles and $80,000 for marrieds.

- New "Roth" IRA that accepts only non-deductible contributions. However once the IRA is 5 years old and the owner is 59 1/2, all earnings paid are tax-free.

- Expansion of premature-exempt distributions from both the existing traditional IRAs and the new "Roth" IRAs for first-time homebuyers, college tuition and more.

- $400 per child tax credit for 1998, rising to $500 in 1999.

- New Educational IRA that permits annual contributions of $500 per child under the age of 18.

- Room and board now eligible as qualified educational expenses.

APPENDIX D

ROTH IRA

This new type of IRA was created by the Taxpayer Relief Act of 1997. Under certain conditions, earnings can be withdrawn income-tax free.

If a Roth IRA has been in existence for five years and the IRA owner is age 59½ or older, no portion of the distribution from the Roth IRA is taxable. The contribution was taxed going in, so it is not taxed when paid out. The really great news is all earnings are then paid tax free.

Eligibility: Must have earned income or
Be a nonemployed spouse of a working spouse
There are NO minimum or maximum age limits

Contributions: Lessor of $2,000 or 100% of compensation if income is $95,000 or less if single or $150,000 or less if married

Partial contributions are permitted if income is between $95,000–$110,000 if single and $150,000–$160,000 if married.

Contributions may be made as long as the IRA owner has earned income, even after age 70½. Every dollar contributed to a Roth IRA offsets or reduces what may be placed in a traditional IRA.

Rollovers: Can't be made if AGI exceeds $100,000 or IRA owner is married filing a separate return. Rollover amount must be reported as taxable income.

Conversions: All or a portion of a traditional IRA may be converted to a Roth IRA. Conversion amount must be reported as taxable income and can be spread over a period of up to four years (if made in 1998 only). Can't be made if AGI exceeds $100,000 or IRA owner is married filing separate.

Distributions: If made prior to age 59½, subject to 10% penalty on taxable (earnings) portion of distribution, unless payout is exempt (disability).

Penalty exemptions (same as traditional IRA) include:

- death

- disability

- first-time homebuyer

- qualified educational expenses

- 1997 IRA residents in a Presidentially-declared disaster area if used for disaster relief

- Certain distributions for some unemployeds

- Medical expense exceeding 7.5% of the individual's adjusted gross income (AGI)

Who are likely candidates for Roth IRAs?

- Anyone who plans to invest in an IRA for five or more years

- New entrants to the workforce

- Traditional IRA owners who have several such accounts may want to convert some accounts to generate future tax-free income

NOTES

NOW AVAILABLE FROM
CRISP PUBLICATIONS

Books•Videos•CD-ROMs•Computer-Based Training Products

If you enjoyed this book, we have great news for you. There are over 200 books available in the *50-Minute*™ Series. To request a free full-line catalog, contact your local distributor or Crisp Publications, Inc., 1200 Hamilton Court, Menlo Park, CA 94025. Our toll-free number is 800-442-7477. Visit our website at: http://www.crisp-pub.com.

Subject Areas Include:

Management

Human Resources

Communication Skills

Personal Development

Marketing/Sales

Organizational Development

Customer Service/Quality

Computer Skills

Small Business and Entrepreneurship

Adult Literacy and Learning

Life Planning and Retirement

7/98

CRISP WORLDWIDE DISTRIBUTION

English language books are distributed worldwide. Major international distributors include:

ASIA/PACIFIC

Australia/New Zealand: In Learning, PO Box 1051, Springwood QLD, Brisbane, Australia 4127   Tel: 61-7-3-841-2286, Facsimile: 61-7-3-841-1580
ATTN: Messrs. Gordon

Philippines: Management Review Publishing, Inc., 301 Tito Jovey Center, Buencamino Str., Alabang, Muntinlupa, Metro Manila, Philippines   Tel: 632-842-3092,
E-mail: robert@easy.net.ph
ATTN: Mr. Trevor Roberts

Japan: Phoenix Associates Co., LTD., Mizuho Bldng, 3-F, 2-12-2, Kami Osaki, Shinagawa-Ku, Tokyo 141   Tel: 81-33-443-7231, Facsimile: 81-33-443-7640
ATTN: Mr. Peter Owans

CANADA

Reid Publishing, Ltd., Box 69559, 60 Briarwood Avenue, Port Credit, Ontario, Canada L5G 3N6   Tel: (905) 842-4428, Facsimile: (905) 842-9327
ATTN: Mr. Steve Connolly/Mr. Jerry McNabb

Trade Book Stores: Raincoast Books, 8680 Cambie Street, Vancouver, B.C., V6P 6M9
Tel: (604) 323-7100, Facsimile: (604) 323-2600
ATTN: Order Desk

EUROPEAN UNION

England: Flex Training, Ltd., 9-15 Hitchin Street, Baldock, Hertfordshire, SG7 6A, England   Tel: 44-1-46-289-6000, Facsimile: 44-1-46-289-2417
ATTN: M. David Willetts

INDIA

Multi-Media HRD, Pvt., Ltd., National House, Tulloch Road, Appolo Bunder, Bombay, India 400-039   Tel: 91-22-204-2281, Facsimile: 91-22-283-6478
ATTN: Messrs. Aggarwal

MEXICO

Grupo Editorial Iberoamerica, Nebraska 199, Col. Napoles, 03810 Mexico, D.F.
Tel: 525-523-0994, Facsimile: 525-543-1173
ATTN: Señor Nicholas Grepe

SOUTH AFRICA

Alternative Books, PO Box 1345, Ferndale 2160, South Africa
Tel: 27-11-792-7730, Facsimile: 27-11-792-7787
ATTN: Mr. Vernon de Haas